BLF
Übungsaufgaben mit Lösungen

Thüringen

Englisch 10. Klasse

STARK

Inhaltsverzeichnis

Aufgaben im Stil der BLF

Autorinnen und Autor

Hinweise zu den mündlichen Prüfungen: Beatrix Kaufhold, Nathalie Schmuck

Übungsaufgaben: Paul Jenkinson (Sprechfertigkeit verbessern), Beatrix Kaufhold (Eine Präsentation vorbereiten)

Aufgaben im Stil der Prüfung: Beatrix Kaufhold (Aufgabe 1 und 2), Nathalie Schmuck (Aufgabe 3 bis 7)

Vorwort

Liebe Schülerinnen, liebe Schüler,

dieses Buch wendet sich an alle, die sich in Thüringen auf die Besondere Leistungsfeststellung im Fach Englisch am Ende der Klasse 10 vorbereiten.

Das Buch besteht aus einem Übungs- und einem Prüfungskapitel.

- Das Kapitel „**Übungsaufgaben**“ ist wiederum zweigeteilt. Im ersten Teil erfährst du, wie du deine **mündliche Sprachkompetenz** schrittweise steigern und vervollkommnen kannst. Außerdem lernst du hier Möglichkeiten kennen, Gespräche – z. B. auch dein Prüfungsgespräch – aktiv zu bestimmen. In den Hinweiskästen findest du neben **allgemeinen Regeln zur Gesprächsführung** viele **Redewendungen**, die du unbedingt auswendig lernen solltest. Mithilfe von einfachen Übungen lernst du, diese anzuwenden.

TIPP **Hilfreiche Wendungen für den Kompetenzbereich „Sprechen“:**

Mit der Web-App „**MindCards**“ kannst du diese und weitere sprachliche Mittel zusätzlich am Smartphone einüben. Auf den interaktiven Karteikarten findest du hilfreiche Wendungen, die du in der Prüfung verwenden kannst. Die MindCards sind für den Einsatz am Smartphone gedacht, können aber auch am Desktop-PC, Laptop oder Tablet verwendet werden. Scanne den QR-Code oder nutze den Link, um die Web-App zu starten.

https://www.stark-verlag.de/mindcards/speaking-1

Übrigens kannst du dir ganz leicht ein Symbol auf dem Display deines Smartphones ablegen, sodass du die Karten direkt öffnen kannst. Auch wird dein Lernstand gespeichert, solange du Cookies und Browserverlauf nicht löschst. Eine Anleitung, wie du das Icon aufs Display bekommst, findest du im Menü der MindCards unter „Icon zu Startbildschirm hinzufügen“.

Im zweiten Teil des Kapitels kannst du das Präsentieren von Wissen, Ideen, Anschauungen und Erfahrungen zu einem vorgegebenen Thema üben, um dich gezielt auf den zweiten Teil der mündlichen Leistungsfeststellung, die „**Präsentation**", vorzubereiten.

- Das zweite Kapitel enthält **Aufgaben und Materialien im Stil der Besonderen Leistungsfeststellung**, wie sie dir im Rahmen der mündlichen Leistungsfeststellung begegnen könnten. So kannst du dein Wissen, deine Fähig- und Fertigkeiten unter realitätsnahen Bedingungen testen. Selbstverständlich sind auch die Aufgaben dieses Teils mit ausführlichen **Lösungsvorschlägen zur Selbstkontrolle** versehen. Einige der Aufgaben enthalten digitales Bildmaterial. Auf dieses kannst du mit deinem persönlichen Zugangscode über die Plattform MyStark zugreifen.

Das erste Kapitel kannst du gut alleine bearbeiten. Für das zweite Kapitel suchst du dir am besten einen Trainingspartner oder eine Trainingspartnerin.

Viel Erfolg!

Auf alle **digitalen Inhalte** zu deinem Band kannst du online über die Plattform **MyStark** zugreifen. Deinen persönlichen **Zugangscode** findest du vorne im Buch.

HINWEISE UND TIPPS

Hinweise und Tipps

Aufbau und Ablauf der mündlichen BLF in Englisch

Die Teilnahme an der Besonderen Leistungsfeststellung (BLF) in der Klassenstufe 10 ist obligatorisch an Thüringer Gymnasien. Mit der erfolgreichen Teilnahme an der BLF und dem Erfüllen der Versetzungsbestimmungen wird den Schülerinnen und Schülern am Gymnasium eine dem Realschulabschluss gleichwertige Schulbildung bescheinigt.

In der ersten Fremdsprache wird die BLF als **mündliche** Prüfung abgehalten. Sie wird als Partnerprüfung durchgeführt, d. h., zwei Schüler*innen aus einer Klasse absolvieren die Leistungsüberprüfung gemeinsam. Im Ausnahmefall kann auch eine Prüfung in einer Dreiergruppe erfolgen.

Die mündliche BLF setzt sich aus den folgenden **drei Teilen** zusammen:

Teil 1: Interview
Teil 2: Präsentation
Teil 3: Gespräch

Die Dauer der BLF beträgt bei der Partnerprüfung **20 Minuten** (bei einer Dreiergruppe 30 Minuten), wobei auf die einzelnen Teile folgender Zeitumfang entfällt:

Interview: 4 Minuten (je Schüler 2 Minuten)
Präsentation: 10 Minuten (je Schüler 5 Minuten)
Gespräch 6 Minuten

Für den Teil 2, die Präsentation, wird eine **Vorbereitungszeit von 30 Minuten** gewährt.

TIPP

Finde dich rechtzeitig vor Beginn deiner Leistungsüberprüfung im Aufenthaltsraum ein. Damit nichts schiefgeht, sollst du spätestens eine halbe Stunde vor Beginn der Prüfung dort sein. Ein Zeitpuffer verhindert auch, dass du in Eile und damit unnötig unter Stress gerätst. Manchen Menschen hilft es, vor der Prüfung noch einmal das durchzugehen, was sie geübt haben. Für andere ist es besser, sich ein bisschen abzulenken, damit die Aufregung nicht zu groß wird. Finde heraus, was für dich am besten ist!

Der Ablauf im Überblick:

eine halbe Stunde vor festgesetztem Prüfungsbeginn:	Im Aufenthaltsraum anwesend sein
Kurz vor Beginn der Vorbereitungszeit:	Nach Aufforderung durch die Lehrkraft im Prüfungsraum die Aufgabe für Teil 2 ziehen **Hinweis:** Du musst die Aufgabe, die du ziehst, bearbeiten! Es besteht keine Möglichkeit, die gezogene Aufgabe zurückzugeben oder zu tauschen.
30 Minuten vor festgesetztem Prüfungsbeginn:	Vorbereitungszeit von 30 Minuten für Teil 2 im Vorbereitungsraum: Erstellung einer Präsentation auf Grundlage der Aufgabenstellung und des beigefügten Bildmaterials **Hinweis:** Während der Vorbereitungszeit darfst du dich nicht mit anderen Schülerinnen und Schülern absprechen. Zudem darfst du keine vollständigen Sätze notieren. Enthalten deine Notizen vollständige Sätze, musst du die entsprechenden Seiten oder Karteikarten vor der Prüfung abgeben!
Über eine Dauer von 20 Minuten (bei Gruppe mit 3 Prüflingen 30 Minuten):	Leistungsüberprüfung im Prüfungsraum: Teile 1 bis 3
Ca. 10 Minuten nach Ende der Leistungsüberprüfung:	Bekanntgabe des Ergebnisses im Prüfungsraum

Die Inhalte der mündlichen BLF basieren auf dem Gemeinsamen europäischen Referenzrahmen für Sprachen, den Bildungsstandards für die 1. Fremdsprache und den Thüringer Lehrplänen. Gemäß den Thüringer Lehrplänen fließen neben deiner Sachkompetenz auch deine Methoden-, Selbst- und Sozialkompetenz in die Bewertung ein.

Die Vorbereitungszeit

Vor der Prüfung hast du **eine halbe Stunde** Zeit, deine Präsentation für Teil 2 der Prüfung vorzubereiten. Dies geschieht im Vorbereitungsraum und wird von einer Lehrkraft überwacht. Während der Vorbereitung darfst du dich nicht mit deinem Prüfungspartner oder deiner Prüfungspartnerin absprechen. Konzentriere dich ganz auf dich und deine Aufgabe.

Für die Präsentation deiner Lösung stehen dir **unterschiedliche Materialien** zur Verfügung. Das können Folien, Flipcharts, Papier oder auch digitale Medien sein. Dein Fachlehrer oder deine Fachlehrerin wird euch im Vorfeld der Prüfung informieren, was euch zur Verfügung steht. Auch **visuelles Material** ist Teil der Prüfungsteile 2 und 3.

TIPP

Strukturiere das Material für deine Präsentation so, dass dir klar ist, **in welcher Reihenfolge** und **über welche Punkte** du gerne sprechen möchtest. Im Kapitel „Eine Präsentation vorbereiten" findest du Ideen, wie das aussehen könnte. Die grafische Darstellung deiner Ideen bringt inhaltlich in der Prüfung nur wenig Punkte. Sie kann dir aber eine große Stütze in der Prüfung sein. Lege daher mehr Wert auf die **inhaltliche Struktur** als auf „Schönheit".

Falls noch etwas Zeit bleibt, nachdem du deine Ideen gesammelt und strukturiert hast, kannst du sie gedanklich noch einmal durchgehen und dabei einen Blick auf die Uhr werfen – reicht das, was du dir überlegt hast oder solltest du sogar kürzen?

Teil 1: Interview

Das Interview zu Beginn verfolgt u. a. die Ziele, dich mit der Prüfungssituation vertraut zu machen und dich auf deine Sprechleistung in der Fremdsprache einzustimmen. Dazu werden in der Regel verschiedenste Themenbereiche nur punktuell angerissen. Inhaltliche Tiefgründigkeit kann in der Kürze der Zeit von zwei Minuten pro Schüler*in kaum angestrebt werden.

Typisch für das Interview sind Fragen zu den folgenden Themenbereichen:

- dein Befinden (e. g. "How are you today?")
- deine Person (e. g. "Could you please introduce yourself?")

- deine Familie, dein Zuhause und Wohnort, deine Heimatregion (e. g. “How often do you meet your grandparents, aunts and uncles? For what occasions?”, “How do you share household chores in your family?”)
- (deine) Schule und (dein) Schulalltag (e. g. “Is there anything you would like to change about our school and why?”, “Tell us about your favourite school memory.”)
- dein Lebensstil (e. g. “What does a normal day look like for you?”, “Tell us about your favourite holiday.”)
- deine Lebensweise und -gewohnheiten (e. g. “How often and where do you go shopping?”, “What did you do on your last birthday?”)
- ein Freizeitbereich (e. g. “What’s your favourite sport?”)
- die Rolle von Medien in deinem Leben (e. g. “What and when do you read?”)
- deine Meinung z. B. zu aktuellen Problemen, neuesten Entwicklungen oder Trends
- u. a.

TIPP

Das Interview dient als **Aufwärmphase** für die Prüfung und fällt bei der Bewertung noch nicht so stark ins Gewicht. Übe im Vorfeld mit Freunden und Freundinnen oder deinen Eltern über einfache Themen zu deiner Familie, deinem Zuhause oder zu anderen oben genannten Themen in englischer Sprache zu sprechen. Es hilft auch, sich im Kopf mögliche Antworten auf Fragen zu überlegen, die eventuell gestellt werden. Das gibt Sicherheit für die Prüfung und nimmt dir die Aufregung, wenn es tatsächlich soweit ist.

Teil 2: Präsentation

Die sich anschließende Präsentation mit je 5 Minuten pro Schüler*in stellt einen Schwerpunkt der Leistungsüberprüfung dar. Du präsentierst die Ergebnisse deiner Arbeit aus der Vorbereitungszeit und äußerst dich zusammenhängend zur Aufgabenstellung und zu den dazugehörigen Bildmaterialien. Stelle dich hier auf eine große Bandbreite möglicher Themen ein und bedenke, dass nun von dir Tiefgründigkeit in der Auseinandersetzung mit der Aufgabenstellung erwartet wird.

Mögliche Themen für eine Präsentation könnten sein:

- dein unmittelbarer Lebensbereich:
  - Familie, Verwandtschaft, Freunde und das Zusammenleben mit ihnen
  - Wohnen (Land/Stadt, Wohnung/Haus etc.)
  - Lebensstil und Konsumverhalten, z. B. im Zusammenhang mit Ernährung, Freizeit, Mode, Urlaub
  - Freizeitgestaltung und Hobbys sowie Wertvorstellungen diesbezüglich
- dein soziales Umfeld:
  - Schule, Schulalltag, Schulpartnerschaft
  - dein Zusammenleben mit anderen Jugendlichen

- deine Heimat: dein Heimatort und deine Heimatregion
- das Leben in einer multikulturellen Gesellschaft
- die Arbeits- und Berufswelt sowie dein späteres Leben:
  - Praktika, Berufswahl und Wunschvorstellungen im Zusammenhang damit
  - Leben und Lernen im Ausland
  - Zukunftsvorstellungen
- Kultur und Medien
- Natur und Umwelt – Wissenschaft und Technik
- Landeskunde/Tourismus: GB, USA und Australien
- u. a.

TIPP

In der Präsentationsphase hast du **5 Minuten Zeit**, um deine Ergebnisse aus der Vorbereitungszeit vorzustellen. Je nachdem, wie deine Sprechgewohnheiten sind, können sich 5 Minuten sehr lange oder sehr kurz anfühlen. Übe diesen Prüfungsteil daher vor der Prüfung **mit einer Stoppuhr**.

In der Prüfung werden unter anderem folgende sprachliche Fertigkeiten von dir erwartet: **Beschreiben, Vergleichen, Kontrastieren und Werten**. Du kannst diese Punkte also in deine Präsentation einbeziehen und zunächst die **visuellen Impulse**, die dir vorgelegt werden, beschreiben und vergleichen bzw. kontrastieren und anschließend zu einer Wertung im Kontext der Aufgabenstellung übergehen.

Teil 3: Gespräch

Der dritte und letzte Teil, ein Gespräch zwischen deinem Partner oder deiner Partnerin und dir, stellt einen weiteren Schwerpunkt der Prüfung dar. Die prüfende Lehrkraft erläutert euch mündlich die Aufgabenstellung und legt euch Bildmaterialien vor, aus denen ihr wählen könnt.
Thematisch denkbar sind die unterschiedlichsten Alltagssituationen und -themen, was euch Spontaneität abverlangt, aber auch Ideenreichtum, denn ihr müsst das Gespräch zwischen euch über **6 Minuten** aufrechterhalten. Die Themen in Prüfungsteil 2 und 3 werden sich inhaltlich unterscheiden, was bedeutet, dass dein Mitprüfling und du euch hier auf einen neuen Themenbereich einstellen müsst.

Mögliche Alltagssituationen und -themen könnten sein:

- Familie, Freundinnen und Freunde
- Alltagsleben und Haushaltspflichten
- Schule und schulische Pflichten
- Arbeits- und Berufswelt
- Freizeit, z. B. Haustiere, Sport, Musik und Hobbys
- Ernährung und Ernährungsgewohnheiten

- Konsumverhalten, z. B. im Zusammenhang mit Ernährung, Freizeit, Mode, Urlaub
- touristische Aktivitäten von der Planung bis zur Durchführung
- sich im Ausland zurechtfinden, z. B. Hotel/Jugendherberge/Gastfamilie
- ausländischen Gästen behilflich sein, z. B. Wegbeschreibung, Transportmittel
- aktuelles Zeitgeschehen in Politik, Kultur, Medien und Umwelt
- u. a.

TIPP

Inhaltlich stimmen die möglichen Themenbereiche in den Teilen 1, 2 und 3 der Prüfung weitgehend überein. Wenn du dich also sprachlich auf die BLF vorbereiten möchtest, bietet es sich an, Vokabeln aus den entsprechenden Themenbereichen zu sammeln und zu wiederholen.

Da es in Teil 3 viel um die Interaktion mit deinem Prüfungspartner oder deiner Prüfungspartnerin geht, solltet ihr diesen Teil vorher in Zweierteams üben. Arbeite also mit einem Partner oder einer Partnerin – und im Idealfall auch mit dem Mitschüler oder der Mitschülerin, mit dem oder der du in der Prüfung antreten wirst.

Bewertung und Bewertungskriterien

Die folgende Übersicht macht deutlich, worauf du bei den einzelnen Prüfungsteilen für ein möglichst gutes Abschneiden besonders achten solltest. Weiterhin siehst du, welchen Einfluss die einzelnen Prüfungsteile auf die Note haben.

Prüfungsteil	bewertet werden	Einfluss auf die Note
Teil 1: Interview	– **der Aussagewert deiner Antworten** – **deine Reaktionsweise auf die Fragen oder Aufforderungen**	gering
Teil 2: Präsentation	– **die Themabezogenheit/der Informationsgehalt deiner Präsentation** – die Qualität deiner Informationsdarstellung, insbesondere die Strukturiertheit und Anschaulichkeit deiner erarbeiteten Präsentationsmaterialien – **die Verständlichkeit und sprachliche Korrektheit deiner Äußerungen** – **dein Ausdrucksvermögen** – deine Aussprache sowie Wort- und Satzbetonung – dein Auftreten, insbesondere deine Mimik, Gestik und Stimmführung	sehr stark

Teil 3: Gespräch	– **der Mitteilungswert deiner Äußerungen** – **dein Interagieren mit dem Partner bzw. der Partnerin während des Gesprächs** – **dein Ausdrucksvermögen** – **die Verständlichkeit und sprachliche Korrektheit deiner Äußerungen**	stark

Erfolgreiche Teilnahme an der BLF

Du hast erfolgreich an der BLF teilgenommen, wenn du die Bestimmungen zur Versetzung nach der Thüringer Schulordnung erfüllt hast. Das bedeutet:

- Du hast in allen vier Fächern der BLF mindestens die Note 4 (ausreichend) erhalten **oder**
- in höchstens einem Fach die Note 5 (mangelhaft) bekommen und in den anderen drei Fächern nicht schlechter als mit der Note 4 (ausreichend) abgeschlossen **oder**
- in höchstens zwei Fächern die Note 5 (mangelhaft) erhalten, kannst diese beiden Noten aber ausgleichen und hast im Übrigen nicht schlechter als mit der Note 4 (ausreichend) abgeschlossen **oder**
- in höchstens einem Fach die Note 6 (ungenügend) erhalten, kannst diese aber ausgleichen und hast in den übrigen Fächern nicht schlechter als mit der Note 4 (ausreichend) abgeschlossen.

Ein Ausgleich für die BLF ist

- für je eine Note 5 (mangelhaft) durch eine Note 2 (gut) **oder** durch eine Note 1 (sehr gut),
- für eine Note 6 (ungenügend) durch zwei Noten 2 (gut) **oder** durch eine Note 1 (sehr gut)

gegeben.

Bei der Ermittlung der Note für das Schuljahr werden in den Fächern der BLF das Ergebnis der gesamten im laufenden Schuljahr erbrachten Leistungen (Jahresfortgangsnote) und das Ergebnis der Leistungsfeststellung **gleich gewichtet**. In den Fächern außerhalb der BLF gelten die Jahresfortgangsnoten als Noten für das Zeugnis. In den Fächern der BLF werden im zweiten Schulhalbjahr der Klassenstufe 10 keine Klassenarbeiten geschrieben.

ÜBUNGSAUFGABEN

Übungsaufgaben

SPRECHFERTIGKEITEN VERBESSERN

Sich in einer Fremdsprache mündlich auszudrücken, ist nicht einfach – schon gar nicht im Rahmen einer Prüfung oder sogar einer Gruppenprüfung. Man kann sich auch nicht kurzfristig – quasi über Nacht – auf diesen Prüfungsbereich vorbereiten. Wenn man in einer mündlichen Prüfung gut abschneiden will, muss man langfristig und nachhaltig an der Sprechfertigkeit arbeiten.
Übungsmöglichkeiten bietet dir der Englischunterricht. Nimm aktiv am Unterrichtsgeschehen teil, d. h., melde dich so oft wie möglich und sprich auf Englisch. So gewinnst du mit der Zeit Routine und wirst nach und nach gelassener. Wenn du dabei künftig auch noch die folgenden grundsätzlichen Tipps und Hinweise berücksichtigst, funktioniert das mit der Zeit immer besser.

TIPP

- Sprich deutlich und nicht zu schnell.
- Frage nach, wenn du etwas nicht verstanden hast.
- Vermeide einfache, kurze Antworten wie *yes/no.* Mit solchen Antworten kannst du keine Gespräche in Gang halten und auch deine mündlichen Fähigkeiten nicht unter Beweis stellen.
- Lerne, Sachverhalte auf unterschiedliche Weise auszudrücken, damit du nicht ständig dieselben Formulierungen wiederholst.
- Versuche die Unterhaltung selbst zu bestimmen, vor allem in Gruppendiskussionen. Auf diese Weise sprichst du über **deine** Themen, hast mehr zu sagen und bist selbstbewusster bei dem, was du sagst.

Im folgenden Kapitel findest du viele hilfreiche Wendungen, die du in der Prüfung einsetzen kannst. Zusätzlich kannst du unsere Web-App „**MindCards**“ nutzen, um dich auf die sprachlichen Anforderungen der Prüfung vorzubereiten.

Aufgabenstellung

1 A *yes/no* reply does not make conversation. Expand your answers to the following questions as much as possible. Before speaking spend a few minutes thinking about what you could say.

2 You are given a short answer in brackets *(Klammern)* for each question. Make these answers more detailed and interesting by adding as much information as possible using complete sentences.

a How do you get to school?
(*Answer:* by car)

b Which environmental issue concerns you most at the moment?
(*Answer:* for example, plastic waste)

c What is your favourite leisure activity?
(*Answer:* for example, listening to music)

d If you could go to America, what would you particularly like to see?
(*Answer:* Manhattan)

e What happened exactly?
(*Answer:* fell off her bike)

3 Synonyms: Use a different word with almost the same meaning for each of the words underlined. Remember **you** are the person talking – this is not reported speech.

a Possible synonyms for *think*:

____

"I think that I'd like to live in a big city. Living there would be expensive but I think I could afford it. I think I'd miss my family and friends, but it'd be very easy to keep in contact with them using social media. If I live in a city like London, I think a lot of my friends will want to visit me! I don't think they would miss the opportunity for a cheap holiday!"

b Possible synonyms for *then* when used in a sequence of events:

____

"In the morning I wake up and then go to the bathroom. Then I have a wash and then I get dressed. Then I go downstairs and have my breakfast. Then I get my school things and then leave my house for school."

c Possible synonyms for *told (told us):* ______________________

Possible synonyms for *visit*: ______________________

"It was funny listening to my friend when he told us his story. He told us about his visit to England. His visit was a disaster. He told us how he missed the plane and then told us about how he got lost in London."

4 When talking you often need to think of a suitable synonym for something. How quickly can you think of suitable synonyms for the following list of words?

(to) shout ______________________

house ______________________

pupils ______________________

(to) tell ______________________

area ______________________

tourists ______________________

religion ______________________

teenager ______________________

the newspapers ______________________

5 To practise pronouncing words, try saying the following sentences clearly. Two of them are traditional English tongue twisters:

a The manager of VW visited the clothes shop.

b Today's the thirteenth – we go on holiday on the thirtieth.

c Around the rugged rock the ragged rascal ran.

d She sells seashells on the seashore. The shells that she sells are the seashells she saw.

1 EINE EIGENE MEINUNG AUSDRÜCKEN

Im Rahmen der mündlichen Prüfung musst du immer wieder deine eigene Meinung zum Ausdruck bringen. Die folgenden Redewendungen eignen sich sehr gut, um in einem Gespräch deine Meinung deutlich zu machen. Lerne sie auswendig. Mithilfe der Aufgaben kannst du ihre Verwendung einüben.

Eine eigene Meinung ausdrücken *(Expressing an opinion)*		
I (would) prefer … *Ich würde lieber …*	→	I would prefer not to … *Ich würde lieber nicht …*
I (would) like … *Ich würde/möchte gern …/Mir gefällt …*	→	I don't like/I dislike … *Ich würde nicht gern ……/Mir gefällt nicht …*
I think/believe/expect/imagine/suppose (that) … *Ich glaube (dass) …*	→	I don't think (that) … *Ich glaube nicht (dass)…*
I doubt (that) … *Ich bezweifle (dass) …*	→	I don't doubt (that) … *Ich bezweifle nicht (dass) …*
I'm for … *Ich bin für …/dafür, dass …*	→	I'm against … *Ich bin gegen …/dagegen, dass …*
I would … *Ich würde …*	→	I wouldn't … *Ich würde nicht …*
I'm sure/certain… *Ich bin sicher …*	→	I'm not sure/certain … *Ich bin (mir) nicht sicher …*
In my opinion … *Meiner Meinung nach …*	→	That's not my opinion. *Das ist nicht meine Meinung.*

6 Join in this conversation about consumer habits and express your opinions clearly. A choice of good phrases to use for each situation is given in brackets together with a suggestion of what to say. Make your replies as long as possible, giving details or examples.

You: How much money do you get each week?

Anne: Not that much. My dad puts € 70 a month into my bank, then he gives me another € 5 a week.

You: *(I think / don't think – Bekommt Anne viel Taschengeld? Was hältst du von der Art und Weise, wie sie es bekommt?)*

Anne: What do you do with your money? I like to buy clothes or things for my computer. But usually it just sits in the bank. I forget about it. What about you?

You: *(I like / I would – Was machst du mit deinem Geld?)*

Anne: If my parents gave me more money, I doubt I would spend it – but I wouldn't say no!

You: *(I doubt / I'm sure / I think – Was ist deine Reaktion auf Annes Kommentar?)*

Anne: Older people always say we've got too much money – what do you think?

You: *(In my opinion / I believe / I don't think – Beantworte Annes Frage so umfassend wie möglich.)*

Anne: Sometimes I feel under pressure to buy things. Do you know what I mean? Clothes, phones – just so that I've got them as well.

You: *(I prefer/In my opinion/I think/I like/I believe – Was meinst du dazu, dass man bestimmte Dinge nur kauft, weil Freunde sie haben? Führe deine Antwort aus und gib Beispiele.)*

7 Mike has just started working in a busy media design office. Look carefully at the photo of him in his office. After reading what he says about his job, express your opinion about it including whether or not it would be for you.

> I work with a lot of creative young people. We don't have traditional workplaces like in lots of offices. We just sit anywhere to work. We talk a lot about our ideas and work mainly on our laptops or tablets. If we are designing something, we sometimes go back to using pens and paper – a real dinosaur approach – but it's often the quickest way for everyone to see an idea and make suggestions about it. My colleagues are great – we all socialise together, play computer games in our breaks or go to the gym for a workout. There's a relaxed atmosphere and the hours are flexible – but if something is urgent or there's a problem, I might have to work until midnight.

8 Give your opinion about the topics in the list. Before you begin, make notes about what you want to say. Use different ways to express your opinion.

a The royal family in Britain

b Looking after the environment

c Living with social media

d The role sport plays

2 ANDERE NACH IHRER MEINUNG FRAGEN

In einem Gespräch ist es nicht nur wichtig, seine eigene Meinung angemessen äußern und vertreten zu können. Ganz entscheidend ist es auch, andere Gesprächsteilnehmer*innen nach ihrer Meinung zu fragen. Die folgenden Redewendungen helfen dir dabei. Lerne auch sie auswendig.

Andere nach ihrer Meinung fragen *(Asking other people for an opinion)*		
What's your opinion/view/reaction (about/on/regarding) …?	→	*Was ist deine Meinung zu …? / Was denkst du über …?*
How do you see/view the situation/this?	→	*Wie siehst du die Situation?*
Could you explain something/your ideas/ your feelings to me?	→	*Könntest du mir etwas erklären?*
What would you say about …?	→	*Was würdest du über/zum Thema … sagen?*
How do you feel about …?	→	*Was hältst du persönlich von …?*
(stark) What about (for example: no smoking in public places)? Do you think that's right?	→	*Was denkst du über …? Glaubst du, dass das richtig/in Ordnung ist?*
(stark, eine Antwort fordernd) I don't suppose you'll/you would agree, will you/would you?	→	*Du wirst sicher nicht zustimmen, oder?*
Don't you think that …?	→	*Glaubst du nicht, dass …?*
Wouldn't you like to see …?	→	*Hättest du nicht auch lieber …?*
Shouldn't we …?	→	*Sollten wir nicht …?*

9 Zoos are quite controversial. Some people think they are cruel, while others think they are a good idea. Look at the photograph of a typical scene at a zoo. Ask someone their opinion of zoos in **five** different ways.

10 Give your view on the following statements about cultural differences and then ask for someone else's opinion.

a Today, almost all European countries are confronted with immigration and asylum seekers. Many people leave their home countries to live in another country. Some people do so because of their work, some do so to escape persecution and others do so to have better lives.

b Groups of foreign workers often form ghetto-like areas. They do this for many reasons: to feel safe, to have friends who speak the same language and have the same culture, or to be part of a community. However, multicultural societies do not mean integrated ones.

c Even within Europe there are many cultural differences. In Britain, for example, people open their Christmas presents on 25th December and they have special celebrations, such as Guy Fawkes Night on 5th November. Foreigners living in a different country always have two cultures. Their own and that of their host nation.

Um jemandem zu widersprechen, werden im Englischen häufig feststehende Redewendungen gebraucht, denn man möchte in seiner Ablehnung nicht zu kritisch bzw. schroff wirken. Einige dieser Redewendungen findest du hier. Außerdem sind einige Formulierungshilfen aufgelistet, die Zustimmung ausdrücken. Auch diese Redewendungen solltest du wieder auswendig lernen.

Zustimmen und widersprechen *(Agreeing and disagreeing)*		
I agree (with you). *Ich bin deiner Meinung.*	→	(I'm sorry but) I disagree (with you). *Ich bin nicht deiner Meinung.*
Yes, of course. *Ja, natürlich.*	→	No, not at all. *Nein, ganz und gar nicht.*
That's a good idea. *Das ist ein guter Vorschlag/eine gute Idee.*	→	(Excuse me but I think) That's a bad idea./That's not a good idea. *Das ist kein guter Gedanke/keine gute Idee.*
I'm for that. *Ich bin dafür.*	→	(I'm afraid) I'm against that. *Ich bin dagegen.*
You're right (about/that …). *Du hast Recht (mit/wenn du sagst, dass …).*	→	(I'm sorry, but) you're wrong (about/that …). *Das stimmt nicht.*
Wenn du entsprechende Adverbien vor *right, wrong* und *understand* stellst, wird deine Antwort sehr deutlich.		
You are absolutely right. *Du hast völlig recht.*	→	You are totally wrong. *Du liegst völlig falsch.*
You fully understand. *Du verstehst vollkommen.*	→	I don't think you really understand (the problem). *Ich glaube, du verstehst (das Problem) überhaupt nicht.*
Wenn du dir mit deiner Meinung nicht sicher bist, verwende Ausdrücke wie:		
I'm not sure/certain. *Ich bin nicht sicher.*		

11 Look at the statements below. How would you agree or disagree with each one? A spoken answer must be given although you may want to make notes before starting.

a "I don't see anything wrong with eating fast food every day."

b "If professional sports people are found to be taking drugs, I think that they should be banned from taking part in their sport for life."

c "Young people today are addicted to their mobile phones. Just look around you – as soon as they come out of school or a shop, they're texting someone. They can't live without them."

d "A big problem with tourism is that it harms the environment. Planes cause pollution, ski slopes damage the mountains, and hotels, swimming pools and golf courses use too much water in areas where there's not a lot."

e "Lots of young people today don't do enough exercise. They don't walk or cycle to school and they just sit at home watching television or playing computer games. They eat too much and drink too many fizzy drinks."

12 In class your teacher shows you this letter. What points do you agree with or disagree with in this letter to the newspaper? Expand your reply as much as possible.

LETTERS TO THE EDITOR

Sir/Madam,
If I had behaved like some of the young people I see every day, I would have been told off – not by my parents but by any adult who saw me misbehaving. But what happens today? People see kids misbehaving and just walk past as if they hadn't seen anything.
Yob culture is growing in our society. What do I mean by yob culture? I mean kids that behave badly, kids who don't care about other people or things around them, kids who would rather drop litter on the floor next to a waste bin or kick it over just for fun, kids who can't put two or three words together without swearing and can't remember when they last used 'please' or 'thank you' as synonyms for their Neanderthal grunts.
I don't mind faces held together with safety pins. Pink, yellow and green hair adds colour to a grey November day. But what does it cost to be nice?
Kind regards, Jane Smith

13 A friend sends you this newspaper article. Read the article carefully. Agree or disagree with it in a voicemail.

EDITORIAL

Poverty is terrible. We should all find time to do as much as we can for the poor people in the world.
There have been many fundraising events organised through the music industry, for example, and attempts made by individuals and other organisations to change things.
However, the disadvantage of fundraising events is that people are happy to buy what they are supposed to, or give money to it, but they quickly forget about the problem they are supporting, too.
Most people prefer to be passive carers rather than getting actively involved in projects to help change the situation. Industries and consumers could do more to fight poverty, however. If industries adopted more fair trading[1] policies – paying people a fair price for what they grow or manufacture, for example – it would help many families that are being exploited at the moment.

Consumers should be made more aware of where the products come from and under what conditions they are made or grown. But it is no use just giving poor countries money. They need help to make positive changes so that they can learn to help themselves.

1 fair trading – the policy of trading fairly with developing countries.

Hier sind einige Ausdrücke, die du verwenden kannst, wenn du der Aussage eines Gesprächspartners zustimmen oder widersprechen willst. Deine Antwort sollte so ausführlich wie möglich sein.

Jemanden unterbrechen *(Interrupting someone)*		
Can I ask you something?	→	*Kann ich dich etwas fragen?*
Can/May I (just) say something, please?	→	*Kann ich bitte etwas sagen?*
Excuse me, but …	→	*Entschuldigung, aber …*
I don't wish/I'm sorry to interrupt/stop you but …	→	*Ich möchte dich nicht unterbrechen, aber …/ Ich unterbreche dich ungern, aber …*
I'm sorry, I don't agree with …	→	*Ich bin anderer Meinung (als) …*
I'm sorry, that's not right/fair …	→	*Das ist nicht richtig/fair …*
I'm sorry, but (I'd just like to say) …	→	*Es tut mir leid, aber …*

Manchmal möchtest du jemanden unterbrechen, weil du eine ausgeprägte Meinung zu dem hast, was gesagt worden ist. Die „Nettigkeiten" werden dann meist weggelassen und die Ausdrucksweise ist sehr viel direkter. Denke aber daran, dass du nicht zu emotional oder wütend werden darfst, denn sonst besteht die Gefahr, dass du die Kontrolle über deine Äußerungen verlierst und dann vielleicht Fehler machst, die dir sonst nicht unterlaufen würden.

(stark) You're wrong there.	→	*Du hast nicht Recht./Da hast du mit Sicherheit nicht Recht.*
I don't think you're/That's not right.	→	*Ich glaube, dass du nicht Recht hast.*
(wütend) Oh, come on! You don't really believe that.	→	*Das glaubst du doch selber nicht.*
How can you say that?	→	*Wie kannst du das sagen?*

Aufgabenstellung

14 Laura and Leon are dominating the group discussion about lifestyles. The asterisks (*) show you where you can say something. Interrupt the conversation and expand what you want to say as much as possible.

Example:

Leon: I don't know why people complain about the environment and global warming. I think it's probably just a weather phase. You don't … (*)

Possible interruption:

You: Oh, come on, Leon! How can you say that? Just look at all the storms we keep having. You can't just say they're only weather phases. Everyone knows that the world's climate is changing because of us – you know, the people who live in it and abuse it – me, you and the other millions.

a **Leon:** I don't see anything wrong with our lifestyle today – we have everything we want and we can do most things …

Laura: But that's the whole point Leon. We can do whatever we want, we've got the money and the opportunities to do so, but what about all the poor people?

Leon: To be honest, where we live most people are only looking out for themselves. I don't like it but there's not a lot I can do about it. I'm not about to give up my computer, my bike or my smartphone just because other people don't have them. I … (*)

You: …

b **Laura:** I can imagine that our lifestyle will be very different in a few years' time. The world is changing so fast. We're already worrying about oil, we know that we're heavily polluting the planet, we're starting to see the effects of climatic change – storms and floods everywhere. I think we need action now. I wish governments were stronger regarding that and forced people to change. Why not increase the tax on petrol, for example? It would stop people using cars! Why not make car parking charges more expensive and the buses free? You've got to be hard if you want change.

You: …

c **Leon:** My mum was telling me about when she was young. You always think things never really change but they do. She was saying that when she was at school, about our age, life was a lot different.

Laura: Yeah, my parents do the same sometimes. My dad grew up without the Internet. His family didn't have Internet until he was eighteen – can you imagine, no Internet till you're eighteen?

Leon: Mum said they never had smartphones either. No smartphone! I wouldn't know what to do. Think of all the times we just text friends for nothing. 'Hi, Emma, have you got the answer to question 5?' – 'Do you want to come over to my place?' – You know, that sort of thing. I really think our parents had a tough life although they never … (*)

You: …

15 Jenny likes talking a lot. Interrupt what she says. Try to select the best phrase to do this. The words in brackets give you some help with what to say; expand what you say as much as possible.

I had a great time on holiday in the summer.

(Wo?)

I flew to Adelaide and then travelled all over Australia. The flight was almost 24 hours long! I slept, read, and watched films, and got bored. Anyway, about Australia: the people there are really friendly and I learnt lots. Did you know Britain sent a lot of convicts there a long time ago? After …

(Warum?)

I'm not really sure, but a lot of them stayed in Australia after they were freed. The White people started to treat the Aboriginals badly, though. Have you heard of the stolen generations? I watched a film on the plane about these children – it was called the Rabbit-Proof Fence, or something like that. Anyway, back to my adventure. I …

(Du möchtest gerne mehr Informationen)

They were Aboriginals with one White parent who were taken away from their families and put into homes where they had to speak English and adopt 'White' ways. They were often taken hundreds of miles away from their parents. This officially continued until the late 1970s but it went on longer. Now, about my holiday. It was really good – the cities, the coast, the animals … and I always bought things from the Aboriginals. Have you seen the bag I bought from …

(Du magst es nicht, dass sie nur über Einkaufen und Besichtigungen sprechen möchte.)

Sorry, but I was on holiday and it was great. I bought things because they were nice. Aboriginals make lovely things but a lot of them are unemployed and suffer discrimination. If tourists didn't buy their crafts, what would they do? That's life! Anyway, I want to tell you about this bag I bought. You'd love …

(Äußere deinen Ärger über ihren Kommentar, „That's life".)

5 UM WIEDERHOLUNG BITTEN

Wenn man in einer fremden Sprache mit jemandem spricht, versteht man leicht etwas falsch. Dein Gegenüber redet vielleicht zu schnell, man wird von jemandem abgelenkt oder man denkt über den eigenen Redebeitrag nach und verliert dadurch den Faden der Unterhaltung. Hier sind einige Formulierungshilfen, mit denen du jemanden bitten kannst, etwas zu wiederholen, das er gerade gesagt hat. Du musst die Formulierungen natürlich an die jeweilige Situation anpassen.

Um Wiederholung bitten *(Asking for something to be repeated)*		
Excuse me, could you say that again, please?	→	*Kannst du das bitte noch einmal sagen?*
Sorry, could you repeat that / what you said about …?	→	*Kannst du das bitte wiederholen?*
I'm sorry / I'm afraid I didn't quite hear / catch / understand what you said. Could you say / repeat it again, please?	→	*Es tut mir leid, aber ich habe nicht genau verstanden, was du meinst (gesagt hast). Kannst du es bitte noch einmal sagen?*
I'm sorry / I'm afraid I missed / forgot what you were saying (about …). Could you explain it again / once more, please?	→	*Es tut mir leid, ich habe nicht verstanden, was du (über …) gesagt hast. Kannst du mir das noch einmal erklären?*
I'm sorry / I'm afraid you were talking a bit too fast for me – could you say it again a little bit more slowly / would you mind repeating what you said, please?	→	*Es tut mir leid, du hast für mich etwas zu schnell gesprochen. Könntest du das bitte etwas langsamer wiederholen?/ Es tut mir leid, das war ein wenig zu schnell für mich. Könntest du es bitte etwas langsamer wiederholen?*

Aufgabenstellung

16 What is the best way to ask someone to repeat what they have been saying in the following situations?

a The speaker has been talking too fast.

b The speaker gave a lot of information.

c You didn't hear what the speaker said because your neighbour spoke to you.

d You didn't hear the speaker because a noisy lorry drove by outside.

e You want a few seconds to think about what the speaker has just said and formulate a reply in your head.

17 Ava is explaining about a township she visited in South Africa. She has also brought a few photographs to show your group. Ask her to repeat what she said about the underlined sections of her talk now that she has finished.

> Last year, when I visited South Africa, I was invited into a township. It made me realise just how lucky we are to live where we do. I'd like to tell you about the township I saw. It was called Mandela Bay or Imizamo Yethu, and is near Cape Town.
>
> What surprised me was that it was a 'town' – I thought people only lived in townships. I didn't think there would be a supermarket there or a hairdresser's, or a church or a lot of other 'normal' things that you would expect in a town. A lot of the buildings were built, though, like the ones in the photos.
>
> There are problems, though, in Mandela Bay; mainly alcohol and drug abuse together with abuse towards women and children. However, education is valued and there are a lot of projects to help people improve their lives.
>
> Let me give you some statistics to surprise you: Mandela Bay has 26,000 inhabitants but it's only about the size of 10 football fields, which means 2,600 people live in an area the size of one football field! Many people want to stay in the township, however, because their roots are there but they'd like it to be a better place to live.

a Wann bist du nach Südafrika gefahren?

Example: "I'm sorry, I didn't quite catch when you were in South Africa. Could you repeat that, please?"

b Wie wurden viele Häuser gebaut?

c Welche Probleme gibt es in dem Township?

d Wie viele Menschen leben auf der Fläche eines Fußballfeldes?

e Warum wollen die Leute im Township bleiben?

18 You are having an interview *(Vorstellungsgespräch)* for a part-time job. The manager of the supermarket speaks very quickly and not very clearly. You have a problem understanding him. Ask him to repeat what he has said where the asterisks (*) are. What you need repeated is in brackets.

Manager: I'll just tell you quickly about the job. I need someone for two evenings a week after school – from 4 o'clock to 8 o'clock. And at the weekends … (*)

You: *(Welche Zeiten?)*

Manager: 4 to 8. But at the weekends I need you from 10 to 4. You get breaks, of course, and half an hour for lunch – half an hour's enough, because there's not much to do around here. You'll be stacking shelves, cleaning, throwing the rubbish away – anything that needs doing, you'll be doing it. (*)

You: *(Was sollst du tun?)*

Manager: Basically anything you're told to do. The pay's OK. I'll give you £4.60 an hour, so that'll work out at about £110 a week. Not bad for someone your age, eh? (*)

You: *(zu schnell gesprochen)*

Manager: I do talk too fast sometimes – even my wife has to ask me to repeat things. £110 a week – right, when can you begin – Monday? Thursday? At the weekend? I need to know for the paperwork. (*)

You: *(Wann kannst du anfangen?)*

Manager: Monday, Thursday or at the weekend – let's say Saturday.

6 EIN BEREITS BEHANDELTES THEMA AUFGREIFEN

Manchmal kann eine Unterhaltung in der Gruppe sehr schnell von einem Thema zum nächsten übergehen, ohne dass du Gelegenheit hattest, etwas zu sagen. Vielleicht hast du auch das Gefühl, dass ein Thema nicht ausreichend diskutiert worden ist, und möchtest es noch einmal aufgreifen.

Ein bereits behandeltes Thema aufgreifen *(Returning to an earlier topic)*		
You said earlier …	→	*Du hast vorhin gesagt …*
You mentioned/talked about …	→	*Du hast … erwähnt.*
Returning to an earlier point/what you said about …	→	*Wenn ich noch einmal aufgreife, was du über/zum Thema … gesagt hast, …*
A few minutes ago you said …	→	*Vor ein paar Minuten hast du gesagt …*
As you said before …	→	*Wie du vorher/schon gesagt hast, …*
Can we go back to … for a minute?	→	*Können wir noch einmal auf … zurückkommen?*

19 What would you say to return to the underlined topics? Use different expressions and expand what you want to say as far as possible.

Example:

Situation: Everyone has talked about their holidays except you. Suddenly, the conversation is now about flying. But you had a fantastic holiday and could have talked a lot about it.

Possible solution: "You were talking about holidays before – can I tell you about mine, too? It was great …"

a The speaker has talked a lot about tennis and is now talking about other types of sport.

b Your friends have had a lively discussion about their favourite bands but you couldn't say anything because they wouldn't stop talking. They are now talking about films.

c Your friend has been giving his opinion about the press. He said they often don't give a true picture of events. He was angry because he always feels he is being lied to. Now he has started talking about politicians. You disagree with him about his view of the press.

d You think that everyone has an equal chance to succeed but your group does not. They have spoken about this topic a lot. At the beginning, they talked about disadvantages in education because of people's home background but the conversation has now moved on. You feel there is still more to be said about the subject but you did not get the opportunity to express your views earlier.

e Your group has just discussed young people being independent. They have now begun to talk about getting jobs. You know that young people in Scotland are allowed to get married at the age of 16 already. You want to explain this and give your view on it too.

20 You are a newspaper reporter asking questions about someone's speech on multicultural societies. Ask **five** good questions about what was said. Begin each question with a phrase that returns to the topic.

Example:
"You mentioned that England especially has been seen as a multicultural society for a long time. Why not Britain as a whole?"

Multicultural society in Britain,

Britain, especially England, has been looked upon as a successful multicultural country for many decades now. At first, the idea of multiculturalism was a good one. That was, to give everyone equal rights and not allow discrimination due to colour or religion. 'Foreign' people were then able to settle and integrate successfully into their new country. But the idea of multicultural societies has had its problems. The biggest of these is that it has led to people of the same country of origin living closely together to create parallel societies; little Indias or little Pakistans, for example, where there is no need to learn English or the ways of the country.

In many of the traditional industrial areas of England, particularly in the West Midlands and Yorkshire, there are areas where there're hardly any white faces to be seen. The local residents speak their own languages and for many schoolchildren, English is a foreign language.

It's understandable why people from the same foreign country like to be together. Groups offer safety and friendship. People feel part of a community rather than alone and vulnerable, as someone on their own in a foreign country might feel.

Many of the early immigrants to Britain are now grandparents and are retiring. A third generation of immigrants are now living in the country. Many of them are happy to be British and are accepted as such. In some cases, though, there's still a cultural problem. In many families, the culture of the grandparents still influences how the family lives. The young people of immigrant families now frequently find themselves stuck between two cultures.

21 Jacob and Emily are monopolising the conversation. Now they have stopped talking, how can you return to the points underlined? Take the opportunity to expand what you want to say as much as possible. (Theme: comics and cartoons)

Emily: I really like newspaper cartoons. They're always fun – I often look at them first before reading the paper!

Jacob: I do, too. Sometimes it's easier to see the <u>cartoonist's opinion</u> than reading a long article.

Emily: The point is, cartoonists can do what they want and no one cares. I've never heard of anyone getting upset about a cartoon – have you?

Jacob: No, I haven't. But I remember reading that politicians sometimes buy the original of a cartoon if it's something they really like.

Emily: That'd be fun – collecting cartoons – especially about yourself.

Jacob: <u>Embarrassing</u>, I'd say.

Emily: Did you ever see Spitting Image, Jacob?

Jacob: No, I didn't. What was that?

Emily: Shame, Spitting Image was great. It was a <u>satirical TV show about people in the news</u> using puppet caricatures of them. It wasn't just politicians, but well-known people as well – pop stars and so on.

Jacob: I don't think I've seen anything like that, but I guess a lot of cartoons have a message. I remember reading that there were lots in Peanuts. That was really interesting.

Emily: A lot of comics and cartoons have hidden messages, Jacob, especially the better ones. Good against evil or role models for the young. You know – what's right, what's wrong, that sort of thing. They're quite clever really.

Jacob: Yeah, we had to do a <u>project about comics in Art</u>. It was fun but hard work. We had to choose a famous person and then given an outline of their life. I took Nelson Mandela. The hardest thing was to draw the same head at different angles. But you don't always need the whole figure. If you look at a comic, you'll see that there's often just a hand or part of a figure in a picture. You've got to remember that each picture is like a finished piece of artwork.

Emily: That reminds me, do you know Roy Lichtenstein? He was an artist in the '60s who painted pictures like the ones in comics. They're great.

You: ...

a cartoonist's opinion

b embarrassing

c satirical TV shows about people in the news

d project about comics in Art

In jeder Diskussion gibt es einen Zeitpunkt, zu dem das Thema erschöpft ist. Niemand weiß mehr etwas zu sagen und es entsteht entweder ein peinliches Schweigen oder eine gezwungene Unterhaltung. In einer solchen Situation bietet es sich an, das Thema zu wechseln. Dabei ist es besser, die Führungsrolle zu übernehmen, als andere ein Diskussionsthema bestimmen zu lassen, das einen vielleicht nicht interessiert. Die im Folgenden aufgeführten Formulierungshilfen werden dir in dieser schwierigen Situation sicherlich gute Dienste leisten.

Das Thema wechseln *(Changing the subject)*		
We've talked a lot about … Could we look at … now?	→	*Wir haben viel über … geredet. Könnten wir jetzt über … sprechen?*
Can we move on and talk about …?	→	*Können wir weitergehen und über … reden?*
We should really talk about … too.	→	*Wir sollten wirklich auch über … reden.*
That's my opinion of (e.g. tennis). But what about (e.g. football)? What do you think about it?	→	*So denke ich über … Aber was meinst du zu …?*
Can we talk about … now?	→	*Können wir jetzt über … sprechen?*
Perhaps we should also talk about …	→	*Vielleicht sollten wir auch über … reden.*
Can/May I say something at this point?	→	*Kann ich an dieser Stelle etwas sagen?*

Aufgabenstellung

22 Change each topic of conversation to the new one. Expand what you say as far as possible.

Example:
food → holidays

> I'm getting hungry talking about food all the time. Before I order a pizza, can we talk about our next holiday now? Your friend went to England last year, didn't she? Did she enjoy it?

a immigrants → emigrants
b British people → Americans
c religion → the royal family
d being a vegetarian → drinking alcohol
e poverty → consumer habits
f global warming → mass tourism

23 In your group, Finn and Hannah are always talking about what *they* want to talk about. Change the topic of conversation to something that *you* would prefer to talk about. This may not be a complete change of subject but could also just be a different angle of the same subject that interests you more. Expand what you say as far as possible.

a Theme: sport

Finn: I like sport a lot. I play football in a team on Tuesdays and then at the weekend I play handball, too. I don't understand people who don't do anything at all. What about you? Do you do anything?

You: ...

b Theme: advertising

Hannah: I hate buying magazines when all you get are lots of adverts. The last one I got had twenty pages of adverts and only a few articles. I get really angry about it. It's not fair – €4 for a magazine just to get adverts!

You: ...

c Theme: respect

Finn: At school it's hard to be respected by other people. Lots of my friends try to dress cool so they get other people's respect – 'Hey, he's cool', that sort of thing. But I think that's just show. Respect is something else. Some people just have my respect because of how they are as a person. It's difficult to explain. But if, say, a teacher tells me off for doing something I shouldn't have done, I can still have respect for them.

You: ...

d Theme: consumer habits

Hannah: I love going out with my friends on Saturdays and looking around the shops. We go into clothes shops and just try things on for fun. I usually end up buying something, though. Last week I got a few T-shirts. One was great. It had 'I'm perfect' on it – that's me – perfect!

You: ...

e Theme: crime

Finn: I agree with the idea of zero tolerance. Zero tolerance is where if you break a law, you get punished. There's no exception to that. That idea was introduced in New York and was very successful. It made New York a much safer place than before and has reduced crime a lot. Some cities in England are doing that as well. If you don't do anything wrong, there's nothing to worry about.

You: ...

Manchmal gerät die Unterhaltung ins Stocken, z. B. wenn niemand weiß, was er noch sagen könnte. Am einfachsten kann man Menschen zum Sprechen bringen, indem man eine direkte Frage an einen Einzelnen oder eine allgemeine Frage an die ganze Gruppe stellt. Englische Muttersprachler verwenden zu diesem Zweck häufig Bestätigungsfragen *(question tags)*.

Andere zum Reden bringen *(Making people talk)*		
Direkte Fragen mit Fragewörtern: what, where, when, who, which, how		
What do you think, (Anne)?	→	*Was meinst du …?*
Entscheidungsfragen		
Are you interested in …?	→	*Interessierst du dich für …?*
Do you want a Europe …?	→	*Willst du ein Europa …?*
Bestätigungsfragen		
The weather is terrible today, isn't it?	→	*Das Wetter ist schrecklich, oder?*
Es können auch verneinte Fragen gebildet werden:		
Don't we all have a right …?	→	*Haben wir nicht alle ein Recht …?*
Wouldn't you rather (have comprehensive education)?	→	*Wäre dir … nicht lieber?*
Shouldn't … / Couldn't … / Aren't … / Isn't … ?	→	*Sollte nicht … / Könnte nicht … / Sind nicht … / Ist nicht …?*

Aufgabenstellung

24 Imagine that you are in a group discussion. Formulate *direct questions* that you could ask to spark a conversation about each of the following topics. Expand what you say on the theme of 'the school day' as far as possible.

Example: "In my opinion, afternoon lessons aren't very successful because pupils start to feel tired and lose concentration. <u>What do you think (Elias)</u>?"

a The size of classes

b The workload at school

c The opportunities that are available

d The use of technology in the classroom

e School rules

f Social life within the framework of school

25 Look at the photographs. How could you get people in your group to talk about the subject of public demonstrations? Give <u>five</u> examples of how this could be done.

26 How could you stimulate the conversation in the following situations?

a The theme is young people's rights but no one really knows how to begin.

b You have talked a lot about Australia and the Aboriginal Australians. There is not a lot more anyone can say. Can you link what you have been saying to New Zealand and get people to start talking again?

c Many people today think that obesity in young people is rising dramatically. Your group has talked about exercising, diets and good eating habits. The conversation has now stopped. Can you get it going again? No one has mentioned the influence of other people yet: parents and other role models, for example.

d Everyone has got something to say about smoking, and it looks like everyone has said what they had to say. Can you think of something original to say about this theme and get people to start talking more about what you have said?

EINE PRÄSENTATION VORBEREITEN

Im Teil 2 der Leistungsüberprüfung, der Präsentation, besteht deine Aufgabe im Präsentieren deines Wissens, deiner Ideen und Anschauung und ggf. deiner Erfahrungen zu einem vorgegebenen Thema. Dieser Teil stellt einen Schwerpunkt bei der Ermittlung deiner Leistungen dar und geht mit ca. 50 % in die Note ein. Für die Erstellung deiner Präsentation hast du eine Vorbereitungszeit von 30 Minuten. Das Beherrschen von Lösungsstrategien ist dabei der Schlüssel zum Erfolg.

TIPP

Um die Vorbereitungszeit möglichst effektiv zu nutzen, solltest du folgende Strategie beachten:

- Analysiere die **Aufgabenstellung** genau. Markiere dir hierzu die Handlungsaufforderung und alle wichtigen Schlüsselbegriffe.
- Erstelle eine **Gliederung** und sammle **stichpunktartig Fakten** zu den einzelnen Punkten deiner Gliederung. Oder:
- Sammle **stichpunktartig Ideen** für deinen Vortrag (z. B. in einer Mindmap) und erstelle **anschließend eine Gliederung**.
- Beziehe das beigefügte **Bildmaterial** in deine Fakten-/Stoffsammlung ein.

Teil der Prüfung ist auch eine **grafische Aufarbeitung** deiner Ideen für die Präsentation. Diese kann dir auch in der Prüfung bei der Präsentation helfen. Wenn in deiner grafischen Darstellung die Inhalte deiner Präsentation gut strukturiert sind, kannst du dich in der Prüfung daran entlanghangeln. Die visuelle Darstellung sollte dabei, wie grundsätzlich bei mündlichen Vorträgen, deutlich **kürzer gefasst sein** als das, was du tatsächlich erzählst.

In der Vorbereitungszeit wirst du den visuellen Teil deiner Präsentation vermutlich **parallel zu deinem Vortrag** ausarbeiten. Mache dir zunächst einen groben Plan, worüber du sprechen möchtest, bevor du an die visuelle Umsetzung gehst.

9 DIE AUFGABENSTELLUNG ANALYSIEREN

Teil der Aufgabenstellung ist immer eine Handlungsaufforderung („Discuss …“, „Speak about …“, „Reflect on …“ oder Ähnliches). Diese Aufforderung kann jedoch unterschiedlich eingearbeitet sein:

Der Arbeitsauftrag kann durch eine **Feststellung** oder **Behauptung** eingeleitet werden. Beispiele:

- “Shopping online has made our lives easier. But it also brings major disadvantages to our environment and economy. Speak about our changing shopping habits.”
- “Many young people dream of living abroad for some time. Comment on some of the advantages of studying abroad.”

TIPP

Diese Art der Aufgabenstellung findet man häufig. Typisch ist, dass bereits Startpunkte für deine Überlegungen geliefert werden. Eventuell ist bereits eine Position vorgegeben, die du vertreten musst.

Der Arbeitsauftrag kann **situativ eingebettet** sein. Beispiele:

- "A group of English speaking guests is coming to your school. You are asked to introduce some typical German/Thuringian traditions and festivals to the group."
- "Last year your class went on a trip to London. Your teacher has asked you to present the advantages of London as a destination for a school trip to a younger class who is thinking about going to London too."

TIPP

Für diese Art von Aufgabe benötigst du ein bisschen Vorstellungskraft. Welches Wissen kannst du in der vorgegebenen Situation bei deinem Gegenüber voraussetzen, welches nicht? Hat die vorgegebene Situation Einfluss darauf, wie du deine Ergebnisse visuell präsentieren kannst?

Die Handlungsaufforderung kann **direkt** erfolgen. Beispiele:

- "Introduce various social media platforms and messengers that young people use everyday."
- "Discuss the role of fashion in young people's lives."

TIPP

Bei dieser Art Aufgabenstellung hast du meist die wenigsten Vorgaben – musst jedoch auch am stärksten selbst auswählen. Achte darauf, ob das bereitgestellte Material dir bereits eine Richtung vorgibt oder dir gute Ideen für deinen Vortrag liefert.

Alle drei Formen können Zusätze zur Handlungsaufforderung beinhalten. Beispiele:

- "Include your personal experience."
- "Refer to habits of your family and friends as well."

Um die Aufgabe inhaltlich vollständig zu bearbeiten, musst du in jedem Fall auf diese Zusätze eingehen.

Folgende Operatoren (Handlungsaufforderungen) finden sich oft in den Aufgabenstellungen:

Operatoren		**Was wird von dir erwartet?**
Develop …	*Entwickle/ Entwirf …*	einen Plan, einen Ablauf, ein Programm oder Ähnliches entwerfen
Discuss … Reflect on …	*Erörtere …* *Denke nach über …*	• ein Problem/ein Streitthema/die Vor- und Nachteile/einen Sachverhalt diskutieren/untersuchen • beachte, dass „discuss" immer beinhaltet, dass zwei Seiten einer Thematik dargestellt werden • ziehe am Ende deiner Ausführungen ein Fazit
Give a survey …	*Gib einen Überblick …*	etwas (meist Komplexes) präsentieren und zusammenfassen
Present … Give information about … Introduce … Speak about … Talk about …	*Stelle dar …* *Informiere über …* *Stelle vor …* *Sprich über …*	etwas Wissenswertes/etwas Unbekanntes/einen Sachverhalt darstellen

Im Folgenden findest du ein Beispiel für eine sehr gründliche Analyse eine Arbeitsauftrags.

TIPP

Natürlich musst du in der Prüfung keine ausführliche (schriftliche) Analyse des Arbeitsauftrages machen. Für das Verständnis lohnt es sich jedoch, die Schlüsselbegriffe zu markieren, den Auftrag gedanklich zu übersetzen und sich die verschiedenen Teile des Auftrags vor Augen zu führen.

"No risk – no fun" seems to be a popular motto among young people today. Discuss the pros and cons of extreme sports. Include how far going to extremes appeals to you personally.

Aufgabenstellung	Übersetzung	Art der Aufgabenstellung	Schlussfolgerung
"No risk – no fun" seems to be a popular motto among young people today.	„Kein Spaß ohne Risiko" scheint heutzutage ein beliebtes Motto bei Jugendlichen zu sein.	1. Feststellung/ Behauptung	Ich überprüfe, inwiefern ich der Behauptung zustimme oder widerspreche.
Discuss the pros and cons of extreme sports.	Erörtere das Für und Wider von Extremsportarten.	2. Handlungsaufforderung	Ich stelle Pro **und** Kontra dar. **Zweck:** Von meiner Meinung überzeugen
Include how far going to extremes appeals to you personally.	Beziehe ein, inwiefern dich das Ausprobieren von Extremen persönlich reizt.	3. Zusatz zur Handlungsaufforderung	Ich gehe auf meinen persönlichen Erfahrungsschatz ein.

Aufgabenstellung

27 Analyse the following tasks.

a Guests from your English twin town are staying in your town and visiting your school. Give them a survey of the education system in Thuringia. Include your ideas of compulsory/optional subjects which should be taught at schools today.

b Introduce a book, a film, a theatre performance or a musical which impressed you.

10 EINE GLIEDERUNG ERSTELLEN

Auf der Grundlage der Analyse der Aufgabenstellung erstellst du nun eine Gliederung für deine Präsentation. Auf diese Art und Weise sorgst du schon im Vorfeld für eine klare Strukturiertheit deiner späteren Ausführungen. Denkbar wäre selbstverständlich auch, zunächst mittels Brainstorming an der Fakten- und Stoffsammlung für den Hauptteil zu arbeiten und im Nachhinein zu gliedern.

Gehe von einer Dreiteilung deiner Präsentation aus: **Einleitung**, **Hauptteil** und **Schluss**. Mit der Einleitung führst du die Zuhörer*innen zum Thema hin. Im Hauptteil setzt du die Aufgabenstellung einschließlich Handlungsaufforderung um. Untergliedere ihn dafür in sinnvolle Teilaspekte/Unterpunkte. Damit gibst du deinen Ausführungen die notwendige Struktur. Das erleichtert später das Zuhören. Im Schlussteil rundest du deine Präsentation ab.
Die folgende Übersicht zeigt auf, wie du im Einzelnen vorgehen kannst.

	Funktion	Vorgehen im Einzelnen	Hinweise
Einleitung (introduction)	Hinführung	• Begrüßung • sagen, was deine Aufgabe ist • ggf. sagen, auf welche zusätzlichen Punkte du eingehst • den Aufbau des Hauptteils deiner Präsentation nennen unter Einbeziehung deiner Notizen auf Flipchart/Folie etc.	Aufbau verschriftlichen/veranschaulichen
Hauptteil (main part)	Umsetzung der Aufgabenstellung	• ggf. einer Feststellung/Behauptung zustimmen/widersprechen und begründen • ggf. die vorgegebene Situation erläutern • ggf. Begriffsklärung	aufgabenabhängig
	Strukturierung der Handlungsaufforderung	• Untergliedern der Handlungsaufforderung in wesentliche Teilaspekte/Unterpunkte • ggf. Zusatz zur Handlungsaufforderung beachten • Bildmaterial analysieren und zuordnen	Wesentliches verschriftlichen/veranschaulichen, Bildmaterial einbeziehen
Schluss (conclusion)	Ausklang	• ggf. eine kurze Zusammenfassung/ein kurzer Ausblick/ein Verweis auf weitere Informationsquellen etc. • ggf. Ansprechen der Zuhörer*innen • Ankündigen des Endes der Präsentation • Bedanken für das Zuhören	aufgabenabhängig

Lies folgende Gliederung aufmerksam. Parallel zur Erstellung der Gliederung wurde diese teilweise für die Zuhörer*innen auf Flipchartpapier veranschaulicht. Dabei wurden nur die fünf großen Punkte des Hauptteils aufgegriffen. Das orientiert die Zuhörer ausreichend. Zu viele Details würden verwirren.

Gliederung:

1. Introduction
- welcome
- say what my task is:
  - discuss the pros/cons of …
  - include how far going to extremes …
- (if necessary, mention any extra main points I wish to make)
- describe structure of presentation

2. Main Part
- statement "No risk – no fun" seems to be … (explain how far I agree/disagree + give reasons)
- extreme sports: explain + examples (with a low/high risk factor, very dangerous ones)
- the pros of extreme sports (explain my attitude/views + give reasons)
- the cons of extreme sports (explain my attitude/views + give reasons)
- how far going to extremes appeals to me personally (explain my views + give reasons)

3. Conclusion
- a short summary of my findings
- thank the audience

Für die Präsentation:

Aufgabenstellung

28 Develop structures for the tasks from page 29.

11 FAKTEN SAMMELN

Bevor du mit der Stoffsammlung beginnst, überlege, welche Notizform am sinnvollsten ist. Hat dein Hauptteil mehrere Hauptpunkte, die sich ihrerseits weiter untergliedern (wie im Beispiel), ist die Mindmap eine geeignete Notizform. (Weitere Hinweise zu Notizformen findest du unter „Ergebnisse veranschaulichen".) Hast du die Darstellungsform geklärt, trägst du nun zu allen Punkten und Unterpunkten Fakten, Ideen, Gedanken, Anschauungen etc. zusammen.

TIPP

Wirf bereits jetzt einen Blick auf das zur Verfügung gestellte visuelle Material. Eventuell liefert dir das Material Ideen, wie du deinen Vortrag aufbauen kannst oder welche Aspekte du auf jeden Fall einbeziehen möchtest.

Aufgrund der Kürze der Vorbereitungszeit solltest du deine Faktensammlung gleich ins „Reine“ schreiben und z. B. auf Flipchart oder Folie veranschaulichen.

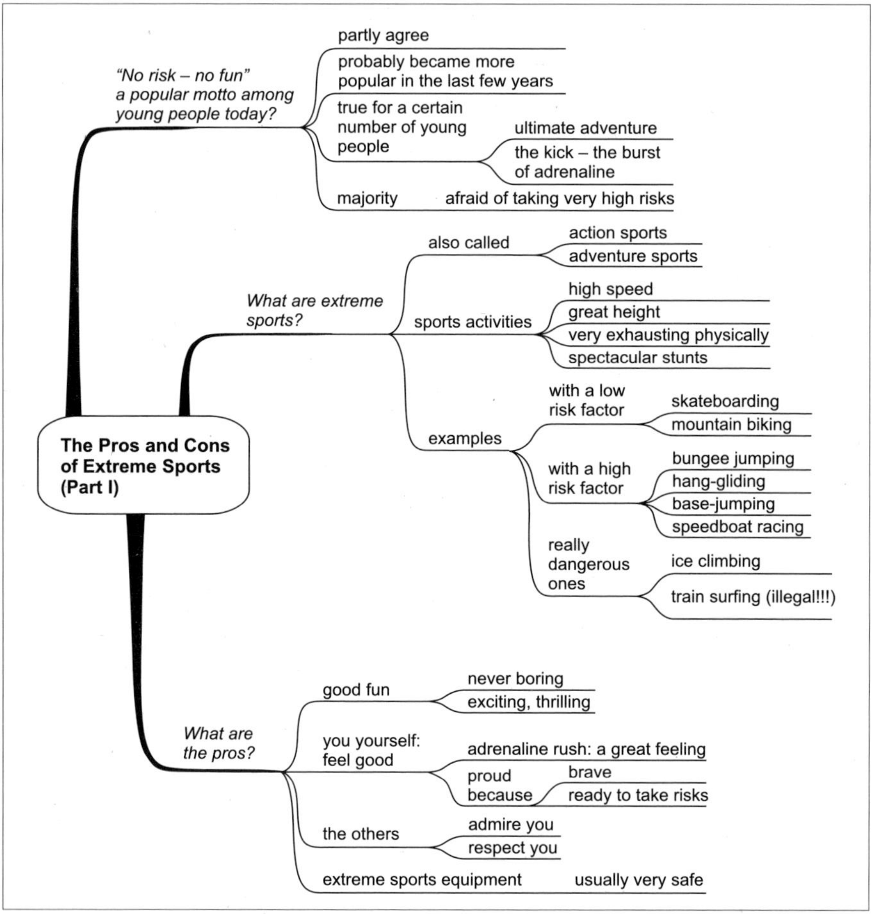

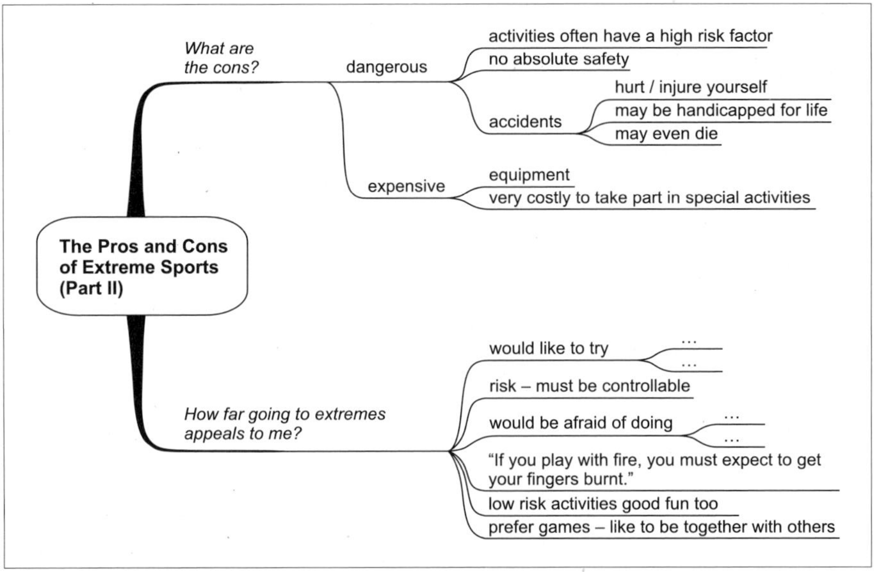

Aufgabenstellung

29 Read the mind maps above thoroughly. Then find suitable forms for the tasks from page 29.

12 BILDMATERIALIEN UND REALIEN EINBEZIEHEN

Mit der Aufgabenstellung werden dir Bildmaterialien und möglicherweise auch Realien (z. B. landeskundlich geprägte Gegenstände oder Gegenstände mit Symbolcharakter) übergeben, die du in deine Präsentation einbeziehen sollst. Finde zunächst heraus, welche Assoziationen sie in dir hervorrufen. Dann beschreibe Wesentliches. Das Bildmaterial analysierst du kurz und präzise unter folgenden drei Gesichtspunkten: Art des Bildmaterials, Informationsgehalt/Aussage und Charakter. Realien beschreibst du und erläuterst, wofür sie stehen bzw. was sie symbolisieren. Entscheide dann, an welchen Punkten in deiner Präsentation sie deine Ausführungen am besten illustrieren.

TIPP

Bei der Auswahl des zur Verfügung gestellten Bildmaterials haben sich die Lehrkräfte natürlich etwas gedacht. Daher solltest du dir das zur Verfügung gestellte Material nicht erst jetzt ansehen, sondern schon nach der Analyse des Arbeitsauftrags und in jedem Fall VOR der Erstellung der Gliederung.

Folgende Arten von Materialien könnten dir begegnen:

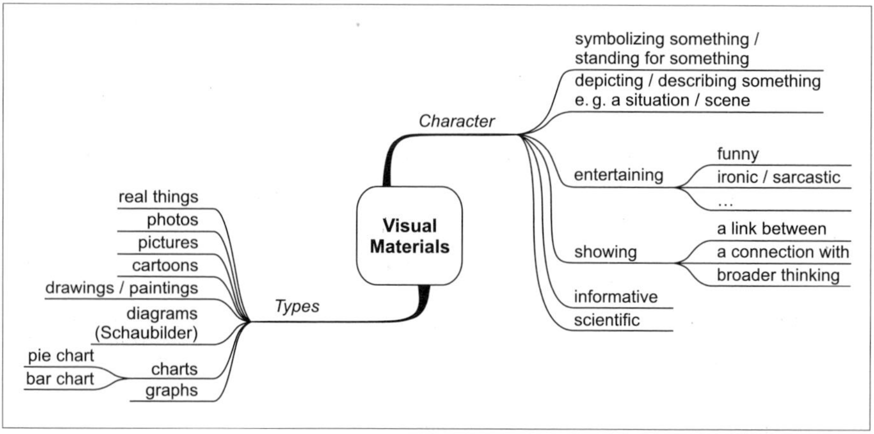

Betrachte nun das folgende Bildmaterial zum Thema „Extremsport". Die Übersicht auf der übernächsten Seite zeigt dir, wie es analysiert und in die Präsentation einbezogen werden kann.

Material 1

Material 2

	Material 1	Material 2
my first reaction	Oh no! Not that!	Yeah, … would be great to …
type	cartoon	collage of several photos
what it shows	a man bungee jumping from a bridge, and looking straight into a shark's open mouth while falling, man – scared to death, huge shark – eat him	young people doing different kinds of sports, e. g. white water rafting, …
character	sarcastic	depicting scenes from extreme sports
message	If you do something with a high risk factor, you should think of the possible consequences that your actions may have. "If you play with fire, …"	extreme sports can be good fun, thrilling, but also risky
where in the presentation	main part: What are the cons?/ accidents or: How far going to extremes appeals to …?	main part: extreme sports/ examples

Aufgabenstellung

30 Look at the following visual material. You have to include it in the presentation you are required to do in task 27 a. Fill in the following table to collect some ideas on how you can include it in your presentation.

Material 1

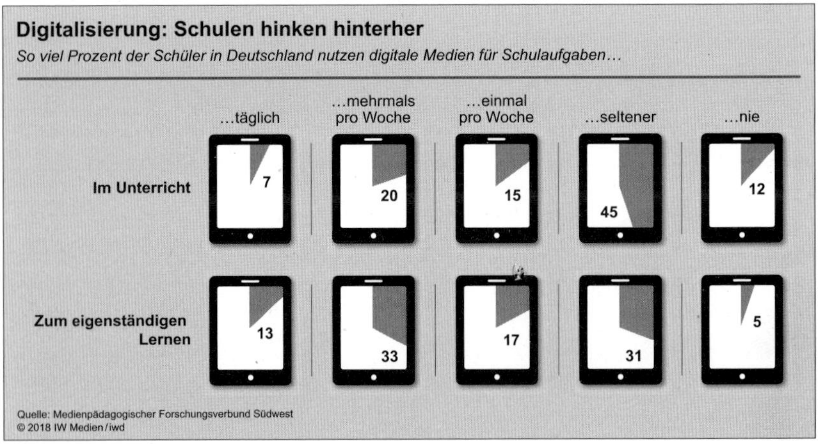

https://www.iwd.de/artikel/analoge-klassenzimmer-400421/

Material 2

"There aren't any icons to click.
It's a chalk board."

	Material 1	Material 2
my first reaction		
type		
what it shows		
character		
message		
where in the presentation		

Im Unterricht der einzelnen Fächer hast du die unterschiedlichsten Formen der Informationsdarstellung (Mindmap, lineare Notizformen, Schaubild, Tabelle, Flussdiagramm, Zeitleiste, Diagramm u. a.) kennengelernt. Das sichere Beherrschen dieser Notizformen wird dir während der Vorbereitungszeit helfen, dein Wissen, deine Gedanken, Erfahrungen, Erkenntnisse und gewonnenen Einsichten in knapper schriftlicher Form festzuhalten, übersichtlich zu ordnen und zu veranschaulichen.
Welche Notizform für das Erstellen deiner Präsentation am geeignetsten ist, hängt sehr stark von der jeweiligen Aufgabenstellung ab. Im Nachfolgenden werden dir detaillierte Hinweise zu einzelnen gängigen Notizformen für das Präsentieren gegeben. Weniger typische Formen werden nur kurz angerissen.

Die Mindmap

Die Mindmap ist eine grafische Notizform und insbesondere geeignet für Themen und Aufgabenstellungen, bei denen es um ein strukturiertes Darstellen von Zusammenhängen geht. Wissen, Gedanken, Erkenntnisse und Einsichten werden auf verschiedenen Ebenen gezielt sortiert und in eine vernetzte Struktur gebracht.
Bei Aufgaben mit erörterndem Charakter (z. B. *Discuss …/Reflect on …*) oder von großer thematischer Komplexität (z. B. *Present …/Talk about …/Speak about …*) ist die Mindmap oft die Notizform der ersten Wahl.
Ein ausführliches Beispiel für *mind mapping* hat du bereits unter „Fakten sammeln“ kennen gelernt.

TIPP

Steht dir für deine Präsentation nur Flipchartpapier zur Verfügung, nutze mehrere Blätter, z. B. für jeden Hauptzweig ein separates. Diese kannst du später mit Klebstreifen/Magneten an der Tafel zu einem Ganzen zusammenfügen. Auf diese Weise schaffst du dir ausreichend Raum für deine Notizen und sorgst für größere Übersichtlichkeit.

Lineare Notizformen und Schaubilder

Lineare Notizformen *(notes)* und Schaubilder *(diagrams)* sind wie die Mindmap für viele Zwecke anwendbar. Ihr Vorteil ist ihre klare, logische Struktur. Allerdings lassen sich hier Zusammenhänge nur bedingt darstellen. Insofern sind diese Notizformen dann am besten geeignet, wenn ein Sachverhalt systematisch, überblicksweise und mit einer gewissen logischen Abfolge präsentiert werden soll. Für Handlungsaufforderungen wie z. B. *„Give a survey …/Inform s.o. about …/Introduce …“* sind diese Notizformen oft sinnvoll und zweckdienlich.

Nachfolgende Darstellung zeigt eine typische lineare Notizform mit hierarchischer Anordnung von Haupt- und Unterpunkten und einem Symbolschema für die einzelnen Hierarchieebenen.

Überschrift/Thema

1. **Hauptpunkt A**
    - erster Unterpunkt
        - – Fakt
        - – Fakt
    - zweiter Unterpunkt
        - – erster „Unter-Unterpunkt“
            - ♦ Fakt
            - ♦ z. B. Überbegriff für mehrgliedrige Faktengruppe
                - > …
                - > …
    - zweiter „Unter-Unterpunkt“
        - – Fakt
        - – Fakt
2. **Hauptpunkt B**
    - erster Unterpunkt
        - – Fakt
        - – Fakt

usw.

Das folgende Schaubild steht stellvertretend für die unzähligen Möglichkeiten, diese Form der Darstellung zu nutzen. Der Aufbau und die Struktur sind stark themenabhängig und die im Beispiel gewählten Begrifflichkeiten dienen nur der Veranschaulichung.

Überschrift/Thema

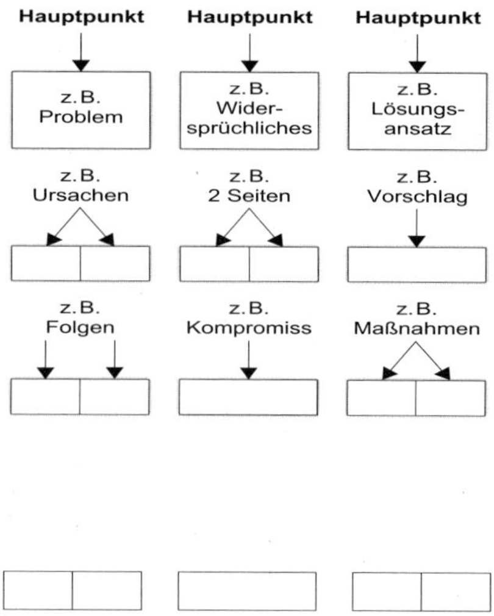

Tabelle

Die Tabelle *(chart/table)* eignet sich insbesondere dann als Notizform, wenn es gilt, mehrere Merkmale eines Gegenstands, Sachverhalts oder einer Gruppe festzuhalten, vor allem in Gegenüberstellung zu einem weiteren Gegenstand, Sachverhalt oder einer weiteren Gruppe. Mögliche Handlungsaufforderungen hierzu könnten sein: *„Compare … / Show the differences between …“*

Überschrift/Thema

	Gegenstand/Sachverhalt/ Gruppe etc. 1	**Gegenstand/Sachverhalt/ Gruppe etc. 2**
Merkmal 1		
Merkmal 2		
…		

Zeitleiste

Nur im Ausnahmefall wirst du für deine Präsentation in der Prüfung eine Zeitleiste als Notizform verwenden müssen. Voraussetzung dafür wäre, dass man dir ausreichend Faktenmaterial zur Verfügung stellt.
Zeitleisten *(timelines)* sind eine Form der überblicksartigen Darstellung der zeitlichen Abfolge von Ereignissen. Sie werden chronologisch erstellt, d. h. beginnen mit dem ältesten Datum und enden mit dem jüngsten. Die Zeitangabe wird dabei in Verbindung zum Ereignis gesetzt, wobei nur sehr knappe und präzise Aussagen zum jeweiligen Ereignis gemacht werden.

Überschrift/Thema

Präsentieren *(Presenting)*		
Introduction		
Good morning/afternoon./Hello everybody.	→	*Guten Morgen/Nachmittag./Hallo.*
I will now give you a short presentation on …		*Im Folgenden präsentiere ich euch/Ihnen …*
My task is … (In addition, I wish to mention/discuss/reflect on …)	→	*Meine Aufgabe ist es … (Zusätzlich möchte ich erwähnen/diskutieren/darauf eingehen …)*
Before I begin, let me tell you how I have structured my presentation: …	→	*Bevor ich damit anfange, erläutere ich euch/Ihnen die Struktur meiner Präsentation: …*
Main part		
How you can start your sentences: I would like to talk about …/mention …/explain …/give reasons …/discuss …		*Ich würde gerne über … sprechen./… erwähnen/… erklären/Gründe für … nennen/… diskutieren.*
Let me begin by/go on with explaining why/how …		*Lasst mich damit beginnen/weitermachen … zu erklären weshalb/wie …*
Let's find out why/how …	→	*Lasst uns herausfinden weshalb/wie …*
Let's (now) move on to …/come to …		*Lasst uns (nun) dazu übergehen …*
As you probably know …/You probably know that …		*Wie Ihr/du vermutlich weißt/Vermutlich ist dir bekannt …*
Hardly anyone knows …		*Kaum jemand weiß …*
It is claimed that …/One can say that …		*Es wird angenommen, dass …/Man kann sagen, dass …*

Phrases to organise your remarks: First, … / Second, … / Next … / Then … / Now … / Furthermore, … / Finally, …	→	*Zunächst … / Als Zweites, … / Als Nächstes … / Dann … / Nun … / Im Weiteren … / Schlussendlich …*
Phrases when giving one's opinion: In my opinion, … / I think … / I suppose … / I assume … / I believe … / I am convinced …	→	*Meiner Meinung nach … / Ich denke … / Ich nehme an … / Ich glaube … / Ich bin überzeugt …*
Phrases when giving reasons and examples: because … / because of … / Therefore, … / That's why / … one reason why / for … / As … / a good example of … / … such as … / … like …	→	*weil … / Deshalb … / Das ist der Grund für … / wegen … / Da … / ein gutes Beispiel für … / … so wie … / … wie …*
Phrases to express certainty, uncertainty and feelings: certainly / surely / of course maybe / perhaps / probably (un)fortunately / luckily / It is a pity … / hopefully / Let's hope …	→	*sicherlich / natürlich* *vielleicht / möglicherweise / wahrscheinlich* *(un)glücklicherweise / Es ist eine Schande … / hoffentlich / Lasst uns hoffen …*
Phrases referring to visual material: Have a look at this photo / picture / cartoon … Let me show you a photo / picture / cartoon … which supports my attitude … Let me use the photo / picture / cartoon … to explain … As you can see in the (next) photo / picture / cartoon … I think the photo / picture / cartoon … perfectly shows/depicts how / that …	→	*Sieh dir dieses Foto / dieses Bild / diesen Cartoon an, …* *Schau, dieses Foto / dieses Bild / dieser Cartoon verdeutlicht, was ich meine.* *Dieses Foto / dieses Bild / dieser Cartoon verdeutlicht …* *Wie du anhand von diesem / dem nächsten Foto / Bild / Cartoon erkennen kannst …* *Ich denke, das Foto / das Bild / der Cartoon zeigt / verdeutlicht perfekt, wie / dass …*
Conclusion		
To sum up / To conclude, I would say …	→	*Zusammenfassend würde ich sagen …*
All in all I believe that … / We should not forget … / … should not be forgotten.	→	*Insgesamt gehe ich davon aus … / Wir sollten nicht vergessen, dass … / … sollte nicht vergessen werden.*
I want to repeat that … / In other words, … / I'd (just) like to add …	→	*Ich möchte wiederholen, dass … / Mit anderen Worten … / Ich würde gerne hinzufügen /* ergänzen …
Thank you for listening to … / your interest in …	→	*Vielen Dank für deine / Ihre Aufmerksamkeit …*

Lösungsvorschläge zu den Übungsaufgaben

Note: In the key most 'answers' are examples of what you might say. Use them as a guide. They are written in a style suitable for spoken rather than written English.

1 a Yes, I do. I particularly like watching football and I enjoy playing handball. I think sport's very good for people because you're active and also because you get to know lots of people. You also get used to being part of a team and all that means, such as having responsibilities.

b Yes, I think it is. I eat it without really thinking about what I'm eating. Sometimes I ask myself, 'What exactly is fast food?' OK, a burger is obvious, but I guess a Bratwurst is also 'fast food' – what about a doner kebab or a pizza? Fast food has a lot of unhealthy things in it – fat, salt, sugar and so on – but if you only eat that type of food occasionally, I'm sure it's not too bad for you.

c Yes and no. I'm not sure, really. Sometimes I think it will be because of all the unemployment in Germany but then at other times I think that if a job is there I've just as much chance of getting it as anyone else. I'll try hard to get a job as soon as I leave school and I'm prepared to move for one – unlike some of my friends.

d Yes, I would. I think it'd be really interesting to see how other people live. An exchange, for me, isn't just about language but about understanding other cultures, even simple things like what's for breakfast. I'd very much like to go away for a longer period, perhaps for six months or even a whole school year. I'm sure I'd gain a lot from the experience.

e Yes, but not out of any thought for the animals that are killed. Sometimes I find myself choosing vegetarian meals when I can. I just like the taste of them. I'm always a bit worried about all the things you read in the newspapers. I don't think meat is very healthy. Did you know that chicken is full of antibiotics? I've read that eating meat and drinking milk can add to the climate crisis, too, due to the carbon footprint of transporting produce, for example, and the methane from cows.

2 a My father usually takes me to school in his car on his way to work. If I went by bus, I'd have to get up even earlier and everyone in the house would need to do things half an hour earlier, having breakfast, for example. If my father can't drive me to school, it's too late for me to get the bus, so I have to use my bike instead, which is alright in summer but not much fun in winter.

b There are a lot of environmental issues, but the one that I think is most important at the moment is plastic waste. Plastic is killing our oceans and takes hundreds of years to decompose. It's something that we can easily alter and the benefits would be great. We don't need plastic bags, plastic knives and forks, or plastic straws and so on. Plastic waste is something everyone can reduce – we just have to stop buying things made of plastic for a start.

c I know lots of people will choose sport, computer games or social media to answer this but my favourite leisure activity is very simple. I like listening to music. And I mean 'listening' to it, not just having it playing in the background while I do my homework or chat with friends. I have some really good headphones and a very good sound system. What I listen to depends on my mood, but no matter what I'm listening to, I make myself comfortable, close my eyes and listen to the lyrics and the music and totally relax.

d That's a difficult question as I'd like to see as much as possible. However, if I could only select one place, I guess it would be Manhattan. I think that's really what America's about – skyscrapers, shops, the colourful way of life there …

e Lisa and I were cycling through the forest and we took a short cut along a small path. We were going quite fast and I was in front of Lisa. There were a lot of branches on the ground and I avoided them, but Lisa didn't see one large one, so she hit it and fell off her bike. She hurt her knee very badly and I thought that we wouldn't be able to go on any further. Luckily, after ten minutes, she was able to continue riding, but later she had to go to the doctor's.

3 **a** believe, suppose, expect, imagine, (to be) of the view, …

b first, secondly, after that, next, later, afterwards …

c said, explained, mentioned, spoke, recounted …

trip, journey, holiday, stay …

4

(to) shout	scream/cry/yell
house	home
pupils	schoolchildren, students
(to) tell	say/explain
area	place/environment
tourists	visitors/holidaymakers
religion	belief/church
teenager	youth/young person
the newspapers	the press

6 **You:** I think that's quite a lot. Most of my friends get less. I like the idea of your dad putting the money into your bank account. Mine just gives it to me every week – on Sunday, when I can't spend it!

You: I like to save my money. I'd prefer to go into town on Saturday and spend it too, but when you get it on Sunday you have to wait until the next weekend to buy something, so then I think, 'Why not wait till next week because tomorrow I'll have more to spend'.

You: I'm sure you wouldn't! But I doubt that you wouldn't spend it, though. Maybe you'd save it, but then you'd just go and spend it on something else another day.

You: I don't doubt that we've got more money than they had. But then again it's our parents and relatives who give us the money. Or, if we've got a part-time job, we earn it. I don't believe there's anything wrong in having more money than they did or how we spend it. In my opinion, older people are a little bit jealous of our generation because we can have a lot of things they couldn't.

You: I think that a lot of people feel under pressure to buy things, just like you. I want to believe that I don't get things just because my friends have them, but sometimes you can't really help it. I'm certain that if I had an old mobile phone, for example, my friends would laugh at me. I don't like that, but it happens all the time. It's like that with fashion, too. If you don't have the right trainers or whatever, you're not cool. I don't like that either, but everyone does it because no one wants not to be cool.

7 I think Mike's job sounds very interesting. His office looks very busy but I'd prefer to have my own desk because I wouldn't like to sit in a different place every day. I could imagine that it might be quite noisy, too, with everyone talking all the time. I'm not sure I'd like that either, but I like the idea that people socialise. I'm against playing computer games at work – that's not me – but doing things with colleagues sounds fun. I doubt that I'd enjoy working until midnight, though. But this is a great job in my opinion and I'd love to do it too.

8 a	**for**		**against**
	important for Britain		
	tourism		too many of them
	stability	**Royal family**	old-fashioned
	focus of attention		out of touch
	tradition		cost a lot
	do good work		
b	important		do more
	pollution	**Looking after the environment**	everyone should care
	government's role		world's role
	organizations		education
	locally		nationally
c	**advantages**		**disadvantages**
	contact with friends		misused
	help if you need it		cyberbullying
	can swap news and information	**Living with social media**	people exaggerate
	easy to arrange things		always available
	can stop loneliness		fake information
	can share photos and experiences		data protection

d

education		**leisure**
builds teamwork skills develops sense of responsibility and reliability people learn to deal with losing as well as winning appreciating other people's contributions accepting rules	**The role sport plays**	fun and enjoyment can be active or passive: player or fan making friends / socialising health aspect: fitness especially for office workers 'work hard, play hard'

9
- Sometimes I feel sorry for the animals in zoos, but then it's nice being able to see them rather than just looking at photographs or films. What's your opinion?
- What's your reaction to wild animals being put in zoos? Don't you think it's cruel?
- I like going to zoos and looking at all the animals there. I think zoos offer people the opportunity to get close to those animals without any danger. I don't suppose you'd agree, would you?
- A lot of zoos help animals to survive. Many of them have been born in zoos and couldn't return to their natural habitat. What do you think about this point? Would you rather the animals be put back in the wild where they will die?
- Don't you think it is better to have places where people – and especially children – can see wild animals than to never allow them to see them? Not everyone can go on holiday to Africa.

10 a I don't believe there's anything wrong with people moving from one country to another because of their work or studies. In fact, I think there are many advantages to this. I realise, too, that a lot of other people have to flee their own countries due to fear. What I don't understand, though, is how this problem is being dealt with. What about you, what's your opinion?

b People from the same country often group together when living abroad. Little Germanys and little Englands have always existed in foreign countries, and what about the Irish community in New York or the Chinese and their Chinatowns? I'm sure that these people did this so that they felt safe and welcomed. But in my opinion, living in these types of communities has the disadvantage that people in them don't have to integrate with the native population. How do you feel about this issue?

c I'm not sure that I would enjoy living with two cultures. On the one hand, things like the Fourth of July in America would be fun but meaningless to me. And what about Christmas, for example? Would I open my presents on the 24th or the 25th? How do you feel about this? Would you open your presents on Christmas Eve or, like everyone else in America, on Christmas Day?

11 a

unhealthy fattening education	**fast food daily**	define fast food obesity social background

I'm sorry but I disagree with you. Eating fast food every day is bad for you. (…)

b

illegal banned bad image pressure to win	**sport and drugs**	cheating punished severely role models accidental/deliberate

I agree. They know the rules and they know drugs are bad for you. (…)

c

safety abuse social communication technological world	**young people and mobile**	why not? texting addiction health risks

I disagree. Some people play with their phones all the time, but most young people don't. (…)

d

damage pollution: transport/ waste businesses	**environment and tourism**	resources controls balancing both jobs

You're right, of course. But the problem is that if there were no tourism in these places, many people would have no job. (…)

e

obesity/poor diet more sports interest reflect wealthier society education	**unhealthy young people**	lifestyle problem technology: cars, phones, computers social background

I'm sorry, but I totally disagree with you. Sure, some people do sit around all the time and eat too much, but most of us don't. (…)

12 **agree:** stop bad behaviour and yob culture/stop swearing/too much unpleasantness/fashion is OK/costs nothing to be nice/everyone should try to stop young people behaving badly

disagree: people should try to stop bad behaviour but not put themselves at risk / don't think yob culture is increasing

I think Ms Smith is absolutely right when she comments upon the bad behaviour of many young people. But it's not all young people who act in this way. Most are really great and do nothing wrong. I'm certain that the problem lies with only a small minority who spoil things for everyone else. (…)

13 **agree:** terrible/help/fundraising/people's memories are short/most people do not care after a while/responsible business/fair trade/consumer knowledge/money alone is not the answer/education

disagree: every contribution is important/people can't always help/people not in a position to change/help should be from governments

I'm not sure that I totally agree with what is said, even though the information given in the article is true. It's easy to say, for example, that people soon forget about poverty, but concerts do raise a lot of money for charity. How much is the individual expected to do? (…)

14 **a** **You:** I'm sorry, but I don't agree with you. Just because it seems like most people are only looking out for themselves, it doesn't mean that all you should care about is yourself. You can actually do things for other people and you don't have to have the latest whatever it is just because everyone else has got one. (…)

b **You:** I don't mean to stop you, but I have to say, I agree. Our lifestyle is harming the planet. We've all got to do something, but it takes governments to make real changes. I think people only react when it costs them money. (…)

c **You:** I'm sorry, but I don't agree with you. Our parents didn't have the things we do, but that doesn't mean they had harder lives. Sometimes, I think their lives were easier – less hectic and stressful. (…)

15

- I'm sorry to interrupt, but where exactly did you go?
- May I ask you something? Why did Britain send the convicts to Australia? It was a very long way away.
- Can I ask you something? Who were the Stolen Generations and what happened to them?
- I don't wish to stop you, but don't you care about the Aboriginal people? You only seem to want to talk about your holiday and what you bought!
- Oh, come on! You can't just say 'that's life'. The Aboriginal people have been discriminated against by us – the White people. And you just accept that as normal. That's terrible – how would you feel if you were in a similar situation?

16 **a** I'm sorry, you were talking a bit too fast for me – could you say it again but a bit more slowly please?

b I'm sorry I didn't quite catch everything you said. Could you repeat it please?

c I'm sorry, I missed what you were saying. Could you repeat it please?

d I'm sorry, I didn't hear what you said/couldn't hear what you were saying because of the lorry. Could you say it again please?

e I'm sorry I didn't quite understand what you said before – could you repeat it please?

17 a I'm sorry, I didn't quite catch when you were in South Africa. Could you repeat that please?

b I'm afraid I missed what you were saying about how many of the homes were built. Could you explain that again please?

c I'm sorry, you were talking a bit too fast for me. Could you repeat what you said about the problems in the township, please?

d Excuse me, could you tell me again how many people live in one football field, please?

e I'm sorry, would you mind repeating what you said about why people want to stay in the township, please?

18 You: I'm sorry, could you repeat the times, please?

You: I'm sorry, could you explain again what I would be doing?

You: I'm afraid you were speaking a bit too fast for me. Could you say that again but a little bit more slowly, please?

You: I'm sorry, I didn't quite catch what you said about which days I could start working. Could you say that again, please?

19 a Can we go back to tennis for a minute?

b You were talking about your favourite bands before – can I tell you about mine, too? I didn't have the chance before.

c You were talking about your opinion of the press, and I would like you to hear my opinion, too.

d A few minutes ago you talked about the disadvantages in education, but I think there's still more to be said.

e Returning to what you said about being independent: did you know that in Scotland …?

20

- You said earlier that multicultural societies were a good idea that has failed. Could some other way of integrating immigrants have been more successful?
- You talked about parallel societies, but that happens all over the world where minorities settle. We don't criticise our little Germanys in South America for example, do we?
- You mentioned that English is a foreign language for many children. What do the schools do about this?
- As you said before, groups feel safe together. Can that ever be changed?
- Can we go back to the cultural problems of the third-generation immigrants? Is this culture clash really that bad and could you provide some examples?

21 **a** A few minutes ago you mentioned cartoonists expressing their opinion. I think making fun of the news is important. It makes people think about very basic aspects of it and draws their attention to them. (...)

b You said earlier that it'd be embarrassing to collect cartoons of yourself. I don't think it would. It'd be fun. I could imagine doing that, too. (...)

c Can we go back to the satirical TV show about people in the news? I don't think that's bad. It's good to laugh about situations and that indirectly brings these things to more people's attention. (...)

d You talked about making comics in Art. I wish we could do that. (...)

22 **a** You know, we've talked a lot about **immigrants,** but did you realise that an immigrant is also an emigrant? If you go to America to stay, for example, you emigrate. **Perhaps we should also talk about emigrants** and what makes them move to another country.

b **We've concentrated on British people** and their lifestyles so far, but **what about** the lifestyles of people in other English-speaking countries? **Can we talk** about Americans now and then look at the others later?

c I think the British see the church and **religion** as two separate things. The church is an institution with problems and religion is your belief. **That's my opinion** at least. **But what about the royal family?** Are they just an institution, like the church, or should we see them as different people?

d We all make choices: some good, some bad and some without realising the consequences. **We've talked a lot about being a vegetarian** as a choice. **Could we look at drinking alcohol now?** The consequences of bad choices.

e **We've talked a lot about poverty,** but **may I say something at this point?** Poverty is not helped by poor consumer habits – cooking meals is cheaper than ready-made ones, for example. **So, let's talk about consumer habits. What do you think about them?**

f Global warming is a problem that's not being dealt with very well. **That's my opinion of it. But what about** mass tourism? **Perhaps we should also talk about that?** Cheap travel means millions of people now go to places they couldn't afford to go to before. That creates problems in those areas, especially in poorer regions.

23 **a** **You:** Yes, I do. I like playing tennis, but we've talked a lot about sport. Could we look at advertising now? You see that a lot in sport but also in other situations too. (…)

b **You:** I know it gets you angry, Hannah, but can we move on and talk about what should be in magazines and not just about the ads?

c **You:** Respect is important, but so is trust. Can we talk about that now? Trust is really important when you're dealing with people. (…)

d **You:** You, perfect? That's a joke! Seriously, though, can we talk about sport now? (…)

e **You:** Can I just say something there? Being tough on crime is OK, but what about children and crime? Is zero tolerance OK for them too? I think children …

24 **a** **Don't you think** that the class size affects children's ability to learn, (Julia)? If the group is too big, there's little time for each person to ask questions or for the teacher to help solve individual problems. (…)

b At times we do get too much work, **don't we**, (Karim)? I often have to work all evening to finish my homework. (…)

c Everyone says we've a lot of opportunities, but where are they? I don't really see them. **What about you**, (Jacob)? **Do you think** we have a lot of opportunities? (…)

d I think computers are very important and we should be using them in all subjects. Perhaps everyone ought to have a laptop instead of a pen and paper. **What do you think**, (Amelie)? Should schoolchildren use more technology in the classroom? (…)

e I think most of our school rules are fair and sensible. **What's your opinion**, (Lukas)? Are there any rules which you don't find fair?

f We have quite a good social life outside the classroom at our school, **don't you think so**, (Maja)? What about all the films and other things that happen during the year? They're really good, **aren't they**?

25
- Demonstrating is often the only way to show people how strong opinions are. Is there anything that you'd feel so strongly about that you'd join a public demonstration, (Clara)?
- Have you ever seen a demonstration, (Jan)? Or been involved in one? Would you ever go on one?
- I sometimes think that people demonstrate without really understanding what they're demonstrating about. What do you think, (Emma)? Do you believe all demonstrators know why they are demonstrating?
- I really don't understand why people demonstrate. It never achieves anything – don't you agree, (Felix)?

If you won't stand up and voice your opinions, you shouldn't moan about things. I'm right, aren't I, (Lena)? You were saying something like that yesterday – about the people who like to complain but who won't do anything to change things.

26 **a** I believe young people today are much more aware of the world around them and grow up much faster than people did a few generations ago. But our rights are the same as those of thirty or forty years ago. I would like to see young people aged sixteen being treated as adults by law and as independent from their parents. Do you feel the same, (Leonie)? Don't you want to be an adult at sixteen?

b The Aboriginal Australians have been treated badly, but at least some action is now being taken to make things better. This sort of situation happens all over the world, especially where one country has taken over another. Look at the Inuit or what happened in New Zealand. How would you feel if you were a young Maori today, (Paul)? Would you be happy with life?

c In my opinion it's not just the individual we should be looking at, it's also other people. Parents are responsible for their children, aren't they? If parents overfeed their kids, they have no chance, do they? If you're ten and weigh 50 kilos, there's not a lot you can do about it, is there? I'm right, aren't I, (Johanna)?

d There's not enough action taken to stamp out smoking. The problem is that governments like the money they get from the taxes, so they never take a hard stand, and they're scared of creating unemployment in the tobacco industry. My opinion is that cigarettes should cost about double what they do now and smokers should have to pay for special health insurance. I'm sure those two simple things would reduce smoking overnight and stop young people starting. (Sara), you smoke – what would you do if your cigarettes suddenly cost twice as much?

27 **a**

Aufgaben-stellung	Übersetzung	Art der Aufga-benstellung	Schlussfolgerung
Guests from your English twin town are staying in your town and visiting your school.	Gäste aus der englischen Part-nerstadt sind in deiner Stadt und besuchen deine Schule.	1. Situative Ein-bettung	Ich versetze mich in diese Situation. und überlege, was dafür typisch ist.
Give them a survey of the education system in Thu-ringia.	Gib ihnen einen Überblick über das Bildungs-system in Thürin-gen.	2. Handlungs-aufforderung	Ich erstelle einen Überblick. **Zweck:** Die Gäste informieren

Include your ideas of compulsory/optional subjects which should be taught at schools today.	Beziehe deine Vorstellungen über Pflicht- und Wahlfächer ein, die heutzutage an Schulen unterrichtet werden sollten.	3. Zusatz zur Handlungsaufforderung	Ich gebe einen Ausblick mit meiner persönlichen Meinung.

Beachte: In dieser Situation kannst du beim Gegenüber kein Wissen über das thüringische und deutsche Schulsystem voraussetzen. Das bedeutet, dass du etwa länderspezifische Begriffe umschreiben und erklären musst.

b

Aufgabenstellung	**Übersetzung**	**Art der Aufgabenstellung**
Introduce a book, a film, a theatre performance or a musical which impressed you.	Stelle ein Buch, einen Film, eine Theateraufführung oder eine Musikshow vor, welche(s/r) dich beeindruckt hat.	1. Direkte Handlungsaufforderung mit Wahlmöglichkeit 2. Bedingung zur Handlungsaufforderung

Beachte: Du sollst ein Werk vorstellen. Informiere die Zuhörer*innen und animiere sie, dieses Werk kennenzulernen (Zweck deines Handelns). Dieser Zweck wird auch durch die Bedingung „welche(s/r) dich beeindruckt hat“ deutlich. Wecke das Interesse der Zuhörer*innen, indem du über den Inhalt und deine Eindrücke sprichst. Entscheide zügig, zu welcher der vier Wahlmöglichkeiten du am aussagefähigsten bist, was Inhalt und Eindrücke betrifft.

28 Gliederung zu 27a:

1. **Introduction**
   - say what my task is:
     – give a survey of the education system in Thuringia to guests from my English twin town who are staying in my town and visiting my school.
     – include my ideas of compulsory / optional subjects which should be taught at schools today.
   - describe structure of my presentation
2. **Main Part**
   - address the English guests
     – welcome them to the school
     – say something about their stay in the town
     – tell them what I'm going to talk about
   - survey: education system in Thuringia
     – primary school
     – Regelschule
     – grammar school
     – other schools
     – further education
   - my ideas of compulsory / optional subjects which should be taught at schools today
     – name (some of the) subjects that are taught today
     – name subjects which should be taught today in my opinion
     – explain my attitude / views and give reasons
     – include visual materials
3. **Conclusion**
   - express the hope that I've been able to give the English guests a good idea of what the education system is like in Thuringia
   - ask the English guests if they've got any questions
   - thank the audience

Für die Präsentation:

Dear English guests!
Welcome to our school!

- Survey: Education system in Thuringia
  – Primary School
  – Regelschule
  – Grammar School
  – Other schools
  – Further education
- Compulsory and optional subjects which should be taught at school today

	Mon	Tues	Wed	Thurs	Fri
1					
2					
3					
4					
5					
6					
7					
8					

Gliederung zu 27b:

1. **Introduction**
   - welcome
   - say what my task is:
     – introduce a book, a film, a theatre performance or a musical which impressed me
   - say what I have chosen
     – the novel *The Da Vinci Code* by Dan Brown
   - describe structure of my presentation
2. **Main Part**
   - about the bestseller author Dan Brown
   - about *The Da Vinci Code*
     – what novel it is
     – the plot
     – what is so special about this thriller
     – why it impressed me
3. **Conclusion**
   - hope that I've been able to give a good idea of what the novel is like
   - ask if they've seen the film version, for example
   - thank the audience

Für die Präsentation:

Dan Brown
The Da Vinci Code

- About Dan Brown
- About *The Da Vinci Code*
  – What novel it is
  – The plot
  – What is so special about this thriller
  – Why it impressed me

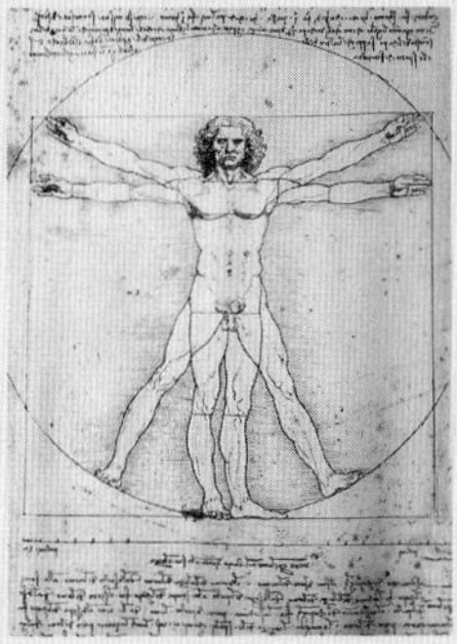

Drawing by Leonardo Da Vinci

29 a

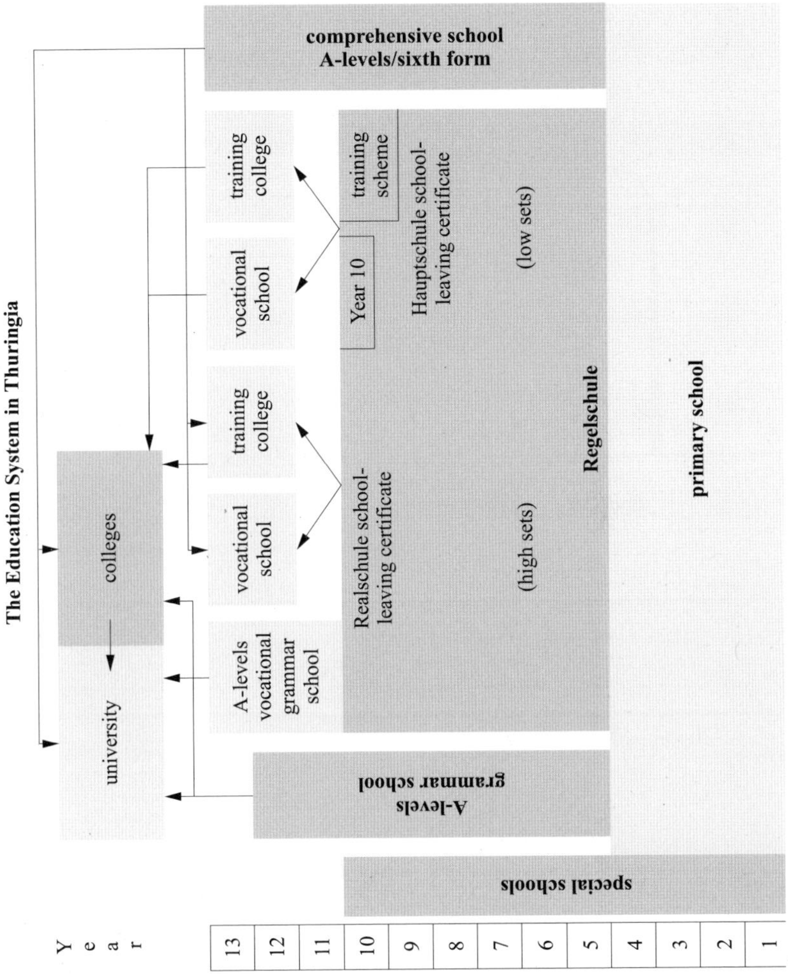

The Education System in Thuringia
comprehensive school
A-levels/sixth form
training college
vocational school
training college
vocational school
training scheme
Year 10
Hauptschule school-leaving certificate
(low sets)
colleges
university
A-levels vocational grammar school
Realschule school-leaving certificate
(high sets)
Regelschule
primary school
A-levels grammar school
special schools
Year
13
12
11
10
9
8
7
6
5
4
3
2
1

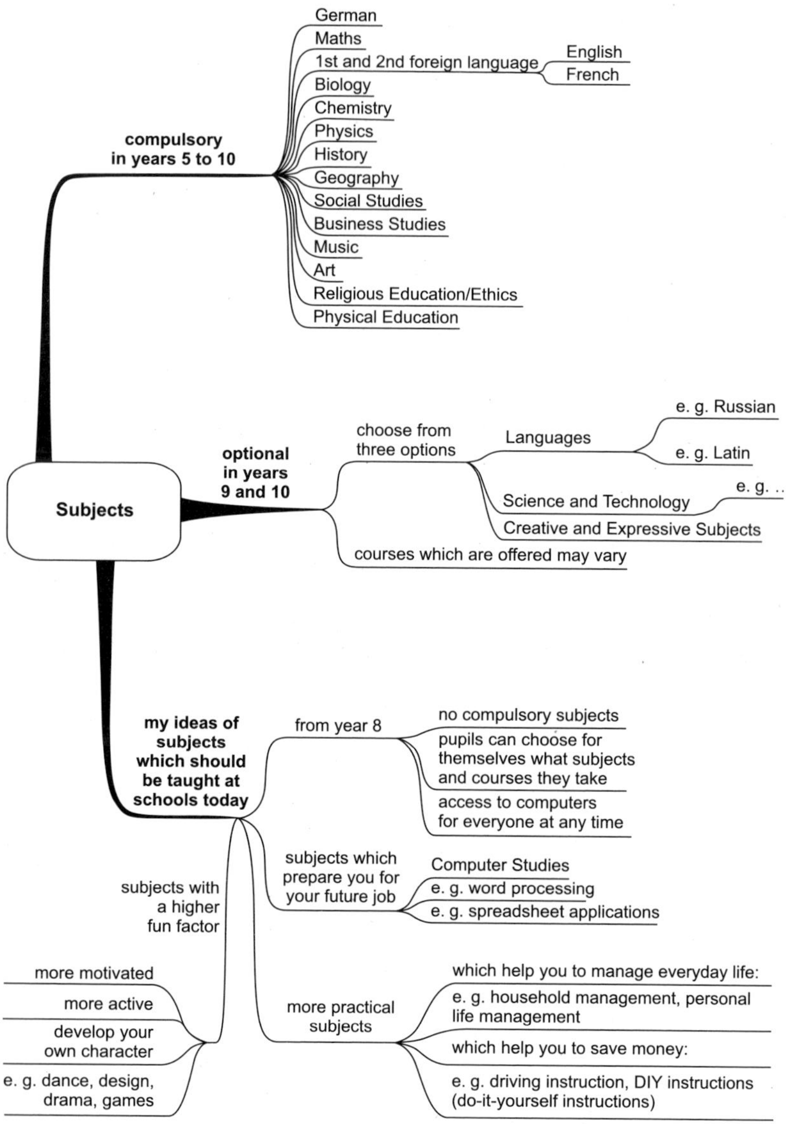
Subjects
compulsory in years 5 to 10
German
Maths
1st and 2nd foreign language
English
French
Biology
Chemistry
Physics
History
Geography
Social Studies
Business Studies
Music
Art
Religious Education/Ethics
Physical Education
optional in years 9 and 10
choose from three options
Languages
e. g. Russian
e. g. Latin
Science and Technology
e. g. ..
Creative and Expressive Subjects
courses which are offered may vary
my ideas of subjects which should be taught at schools today
from year 8
no compulsory subjects
pupils can choose for themselves what subjects and courses they take
access to computers for everyone at any time
subjects which prepare you for your future job
Computer Studies
e. g. word processing
e. g. spreadsheet applications
more practical subjects
which help you to manage everyday life:
e. g. household management, personal life management
which help you to save money:
e. g. driving instruction, DIY instructions (do-it-yourself instructions)
subjects with a higher fun factor
more motivated
more active
develop your own character
e. g. dance, design, drama, games

b **About Dan Brown**

- an American author of thrillers
- before he became famous as a writer: songwriter, pop singer, English teacher
- bestsellers in the last ten years
  - *Digital Fortress (Diabolus)*
  - *Angels and Demons (Illuminati)*
  - *The Da Vinci Code* – most famous one

***The Da Vinci Code* – What kind of novel it is**

- a high-energy thriller, not simply a detective story or a murder hunt
- a brilliant mixture of
  - crime, mythology and little-known historical facts,
  - an incredible analysis of *The Last Supper* by Da Vinci and
  - shocking interpretations of Catholic legends

The plot	What is so special about this thriller	Why it impressed me
• a strange murder in the Louvre in Paris • French Police call in the American professor Robert Langdon (an expert on ancient symbols) • Sophie Neveu (granddaughter of the murder victim) joins Langdon • want to solve the mysterious secret that died with Sophie's grandfather • thrilling treasure hunt begins • follow the hero and heroine on their exciting chase from one clue to the next • during their treasure hunt they have to deal with: – ancient mythology – secret society – the legends of Christianity	• once you have started it, you will not be able to put it down, I am sure • I simply could not stop reading • author always leads reader to a new mystery • impressive historical or scientific facts are revealed • Da Vinci's painting *The Last Supper:* the disciple next to Jesus is seen as a woman – Mary Magdalene • novel sets you thinking • forces you to decide what you're reading: a piece of dubious fiction or the plain truth	• entertaining from the first page to the last • good fun • many amazing facts and clever fictional ideas impressed me deeply • author grabs your attention brilliantly • you think: *Incredible! How amazing!* or *No! I can't believe that!* • surprised or even shocked at what you are reading • must form your own opinion – never easy

- recommend *The Da Vinci Code* to anyone who likes a good mixture of suspense, history and mythology, amazing facts and dubious fiction
- all the time: novel challenges you to think and decide for yourself

30			
	my first reaction	**1**	hard to believe …
		2	My goodness …
	type	**1**	bar chart
		2	cartoon
	what it shows	**1**	• results of a survey about digitalization at schools done in 2018 • topic: comparison of how often pupils use digital media for learning at home and in classroom
		2	• a junior pupil in class who doesn't know how to use a blackboard and chalk • seems to be looking for icons to click • poster next to the blackboard reads: "Reading is cool"
	character	**1**	informative
		2	funny
	message	**1**	• digital media is rarely used for learning in schools • at home students frequently use digital media to study • conclusion: teachers should include digital media more often to improve learning effects • subjects like media competence, coding and programming have to be a regular part of the Thuringian curriculum
		2	• schools are not always up-to-date when it comes to technological equipment • (small) children are confronted with technological devices in their everyday lives and thus expect them to be part of their school experience
	where in the presentation	**1**	main part: my ideas of compulsory/optional subjects which should be taught at school
		2	main part: my ideas of compulsory/ optional subjects which should be taught at school

IM STIL DER BLF

Aufgaben im Stil der BLF

Übungsaufgabe 1

PART 1: INTERVIEW

Teacher:
Good morning/afternoon. Welcome to your oral assessment. I hope you're fine. This is my colleague Mrs Peter. She's just observing your performance. Please introduce yourselves.

Julie, tell us a bit about the town/village you are from.
And what about you, Moritz?

Julie: ...
Moritz: ...

Moritz, what do you like about living in your home town/village?
What about you, Julie?

Moritz: ...
Julie: ...

Julie, what leisure activities can you do in your home town/village?
And what about the place where you live, Moritz?

Julie: ...
Moritz: ...

Moritz, how do you spend your free time?
And you, Julie?

Moritz: ...
Julie: ...

PART 2: PRESENTATION

Discuss the advantages and disadvantages of living in a big city. Include the following material.

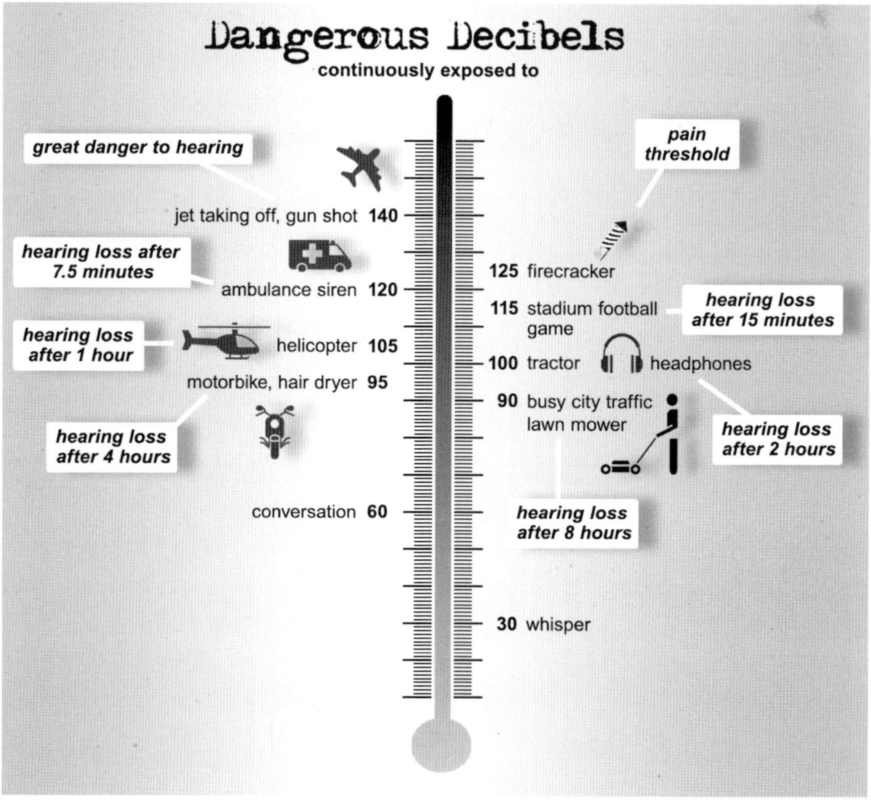

PART 3: TALK

Teacher:
Now Julie and Moritz, I'd like the two of you to talk about a topic for about 6 minutes.
You will get some material to help you.
Now listen to your task carefully.

Here are some pictures which show you different forms of housing. Say which forms of housing you can see in the pictures and describe them. Then talk about the advantages and disadvantages of living there. Decide which you would prefer.

Picture 1

Picture 2

Picture 3

Picture 4

Lösungsvorschläge

TIPP

- Die stichpunktartigen Lösungen sind lediglich Vorschläge. Nicht alle Punkte und Bilder müssen in deine Präsentation eingebracht werden oder im Gespräch vorkommen.
- Stoppe beim Üben die Zeit, damit du weißt, wie viele Informationen du wirklich benötigst. Auch in der Prüfung solltest du die Uhr im Blick behalten, denn nach 5 Minuten (Präsentation) bzw. 6 Minuten (Gespräch) wird der Prüfer oder die Prüferin dich/euch unterbrechen.
- Wenn du merkst, dass die Zeit bald um ist, bemühe dich um einen Schlusssatz oder eine Zusammenfassung, damit die Präsentation bzw. das Gespräch einen runden Schluss finden.
- Bevor du mit dem Üben beginnst, überlege dir 3–5 *useful phrases*, die du einbauen möchtest, um deinen Ausdruck zu verbessern. Du findest sie in den Kapiteln im vorderen Teil des Buches.

PART 1: INTERVIEW

Good morning/afternoon. Welcome to your oral assessment. I hope you're fine. This is my colleague Mrs Peter. She's just observing your performance. Please introduce yourselves.
My name's Julie and I'm 16 years old. I'm from Gotha. I'm a pupil at Arnoldi Grammar School and I'm in Year 10.

Julie, tell us a bit about the town/village you are from.
As you already know, I'm from Gotha. It's a nice little town in the federal state of Thuringia. Gotha is one of the oldest towns in Germany. Its beginnings go back to the 8th century. Gotha used to be an important town and was even a capital from the 17th to the early 20th century. Today Gotha is a modern town with a population of about 47,000. There are some cultural attractions, like Friedenstein Castle. It houses famous art collections and the Ekhof Theatre.

[Moritz, what do you like about living in your hometown/village?] And you, Julie?
First of all, I like the town's character and atmosphere. It's a nice little town and I love the old part of town with its historical buildings. There's rarely a hectic or noisy atmosphere in the city centre and shopping there is good fun. Another thing I like is the good transport system in and around the town. It's quite easy to get from A to B and the "Thüringerwaldbahn" even takes you to popular places in the Thuringian Forest.

Julie, what leisure activities can you do in your hometown/village?
There are lots of things you can do in and around Gotha, from cultural activities to sports and just being outdoors. There is something for everyone. You can go to the theatre or to concerts. There are cinemas, discos and youth clubs. You can go swimming and bowling, play tennis or watch horse racing. For those who like being outdoors there is a zoo and there are some popular places for outings nearby.

[Moritz, how do you spend your free time?] And you, Julie?
Well, I'm a football fan and I spend a lot of time playing or watching football. I go to football training twice a week. I'm on the junior team of the FSV Wacker 03 and there are often matches at the weekend. I spend the rest of my free time at home watching TV or videos, listening to music, reading and surfing the Internet, or I meet my friends.

PART 2: PRESENTATION

Loud, noisy, full of people – but also rich in culture. In this presentation I will talk about living in big cities and discuss the pros and cons of that. Before I begin, let me explain the structure of my presentation.

Advantages:

1. The best of everything
2. Better opportunities as regards jobs and careers

Disadvantages:

3. Hectic activity and noise
4. Serious problems
5. Expensive to live there

Let's begin …

Advantages:

1. The best of everything
   - Lots of entertainment facilities (e. g. theatres, concert halls, cinemas, amusement arcades and stadiums)
   - Young people – can do quite a number of things (e. g. live concerts, latest films, fantastic discos or all kinds of sport and hobbies)
   - Photo of New York
     - Manhattan with its skyscrapers
     - Many famous landmarks, tourist attractions and museums (e. g. the Statue of Liberty, the Empire State Building, Broadway with its theatres, the Museum of Modern Art or Central Park)
     - People often say: New York – the city that never sleeps
     - Nightlife – fantastic

2. Better opportunities as regards jobs and careers
   - Usually lots of different educational institutions (e. g. colleges and universities)
   - Better chances of
     - Getting excellent qualifications and a good and/or interesting job
     - Earning a lot of money
   - Photo of New York
     - Manhattan – a major commercial and financial centre of the United States
     - Must be exciting to work there

Disadvantages:

3. Hectic activity and noise (diagram)
   - The impact of noise on your hearing
   - Busy city traffic
     - About 90 decibels in volume
     - If continuously exposed to the noise of city traffic – suffer from hearing loss after only 8 hours
   - Noise from a helicopter or an ambulance siren
     - Hearing suffers after only one hour or even 7.5 minutes
   - A jet taking off
     - Volume of noise about 140 decibels
     - Aircraft noise poses great danger to your hearing
   - Motor vehicle noise and aircraft noise – quite typical of big cities
4. Serious problems
   (crime, poverty, unemployment, homelessness, drug trafficking and prostitution)
5. Expensive to live there
   - Enjoying the exciting things is expensive
   - If poor/not have the money, life very boring and uninteresting there, too
   - Expensive rents

Let me close by saying that living in a big city and living in the country both have their advantages, but they also have their disadvantages. People who do not mind noise, hectic activity and pollution will prefer city life. But I personally feel more at home in a small town or village.

Example:

Hello everybody! I would like to welcome you to my presentation. My task is to discuss the advantages and disadvantages of living in a big city.

First let me say a few words on the structure of my presentation. I will begin with the advantages of living in a big city. I will talk about the fact that cities usually have the best of everything. Then I will discuss why you have better opportunities in big places. Second, I will speak about the disadvantages of living in a big city. I will talk about the fact that cities are usually full of hectic activity and noise. Next, I will mention serious problems that are often typical of large places. And finally, I will discuss the fact that living in a big city is expensive.

Many people – especially young people – usually think that living in a big city must be fantastic. Teenagers often want to live in large towns or cities because they think that life in the country is boring. But in my opinion, living in large places does not only have advantages. It has disadvantages as well.

But first, let me talk about the advantages of life in a big city. I believe the most important advantage is that cities have the best of everything. There are generally lots of places offering entertainment, like theatres, concert halls, cinemas, amusement arcades and stadiums. Second, young people can do quite a number of different things there: go to live concerts, watch the latest films, go to fantastic discos or do all kinds of sport and hobbies. Have a look at this photo of New York. It shows Manhattan with its skyscrapers. Unfortunately, I haven't been to New York myself yet, but from my English lessons I know that Manhattan has many famous landmarks, tourist attractions and museums: the Statue of Liberty, the Empire State Building, Broadway with its theatres and the Museum of Modern Art, Central Park, to name just a few. People often say that New York is the city that never sleeps. The nightlife must be fantastic there, I'm sure.

Furthermore, another advantage of big cities is that there are usually lots of different educational institutions there, like colleges and universities. I think in large places you have a better chance of getting excellent qualifications, finding a good or interesting job and earning a lot of money. Have a look at the photo of New York again. Manhattan is a major commercial and financial centre of the United States. It must be exciting to work there.

On the other hand, however, I am convinced that living in huge places also has its disadvantages. First of all, metropolises like New York or London or even Berlin are full of hectic activity and noise. Let's have a look at this diagram. It shows the impact of noise on your hearing in a very informative way. For example, busy city traffic is about 90 decibels in volume. If you are continuously exposed to the noise of city traffic, you suffer from hearing loss after only eight hours. The noise from a helicopter or an ambulance siren is even worse. If you are continuously exposed to these noises, your hearing suffers after only one hour or even 7.5 minutes. When a jet takes off, the volume of noise is about 140 decibels. Therefore, aircraft noise poses great danger to your hearing. But noise from motor vehicles and aircraft is quite typical of big cities, isn't it?

Second, in my opinion big towns and cities usually have a lot of problems like crime, poverty, unemployment, homelessness, drug trafficking and prostitution. Moreover, life in a big city is very expensive. The rents are high and you can only enjoy the exciting things if you have enough money. If you are poor and don't have the money, on the other hand, life can be very boring there, too.

Let me close by saying that living in a big city and living in the country both have their advantages, but they also have their disadvantages. People who don't mind noise, hectic activity and pollution will prefer city life. But I personally feel more at home in a small town or village.

That was my presentation on the advantages and disadvantages of living in a big city. Thank you for your attention.

PART 3: TALK

TIPP

Da im Gespräch auch dein Interagieren mit deinem Mitprüfling bewertet wird, solltest du dich ganz bewusst bemühen, immer wieder den Bezug zu deinem Partner bzw. deiner Partnerin herzustellen und an die Aussagen anzuknüpfen.

Things you could talk about

Describe the houses:

- **Picture 1:** probably privately owned, big detached house, quite new and modern, nice front and a small garden, American style, several big windows, a balcony on the upper floor, veranda downstairs
- **Picture 2:** probably privately owned, terraced houses, typically British, a bit older and rather small, only two windows and a small porch, tiny front garden
- **Picture 3:** tower block, probably flats for rent, lots of windows and balconies (which all look the same), a garden with trees, not very attractive
- **Picture 4:** old blocks of flats, probably for rent, different windows and balconies, some of the buildings may have been renovated, road and river in front of them, probably good view

Compare possible rents and living conditions:

- Rent in the building by the river probably higher, possibly fashionable area
- Flats in tower blocks are usually very small (tiny kitchen, bathroom, etc.), but the rent is lower (only alternative for people with a low income, students and trainees)
- Terraced houses are also often smaller, you live closer to your neighbours, they can be found in the city
- Detached houses are normally more expensive and are usually located in the suburbs or in towns or villages

Discuss possibility of buying/building a house:

- Building from scratch may be more expensive than renovating
- But it is also more possible to make the house fit your needs

Decide which you would prefer.

Aufgaben im Stil der BLF
Übungsaufgabe 2

PART 1: INTERVIEW

Teacher:
Good morning/afternoon. Welcome to your oral assessment. I hope you're fine. This is my colleague Mr Nguyen. He's just observing your performance. Please introduce yourselves.

Chiara, tell us a bit about your family.
And what about your family, Vanessa?

Chiara: ...
Vanessa: ...

Vanessa, how do you share the housework?
And you, Chiara?

Vanessa: ...
Chiara: ...

Chiara, how important is it for you and your parents to have meals together as a family?
Vanessa, is that true for your family, too?

Chiara: ...
Vanessa: ...

Vanessa, how does your family celebrate festivities like Easter or Christmas?
And how does your family spend those times, Chiara?

Vanessa: ...
Chiara: ...

PART 2: PRESENTATION

You often hear people say that we eat too much fatty and sweet food, but not enough health food. Is that true for you? Reflect on your eating habits. Also explain what eating a healthy balanced diet means.
Include the following material.

PART 3: TALK

Teacher:
Now Chiara and Vanessa, I'd like the two of you to talk about a topic for about 6 minutes. You will get some material to help you.
Now listen to your task carefully.

Here is some material which shows you parts of menus. Talk about the food you can have at the different places. Say which place you would prefer for eating out. Agree on one of them.

Olive Garden Italian Restaurant
Italian Specialities
Make dinner a real event and experience our Italian specialities by exploring our enticing Olive Garden dinner menu. Buon Appetito!
appetizers .... 3.95 – 5.95
soups and salads .... 4.95 – 5.95
pizzas .... 5.50 – 6.95
classic recipes .... 7.95 – 10.95
beef and pork .... 8.50 – 12.95
filled pastas .... 6.95 – 7.95
chicken .... 4.50 – 5.95
fish and sea food .... 7.50 – 9.50

RUTH'S STEAK HOUSE
Our famous steaks are seared to perfection at 1800 degrees and topped with fresh butter so they sizzle all the way to your table
APPETIZERS AND SOUPS
SALADS AND SIDES
STEAKS
WINE AND COCKTAILS
DESSERT

Hamburger
3.65
Cheeseburger
3.45
Chicken Nuggets
2.95
Tasty Burger
2.95
Quarter Pounder
3.95
Caesar Salad
1.95
French Fries (small, medium, large)
1.65
Icecream
1.45
Cookies
2.55
Shakes
2.95

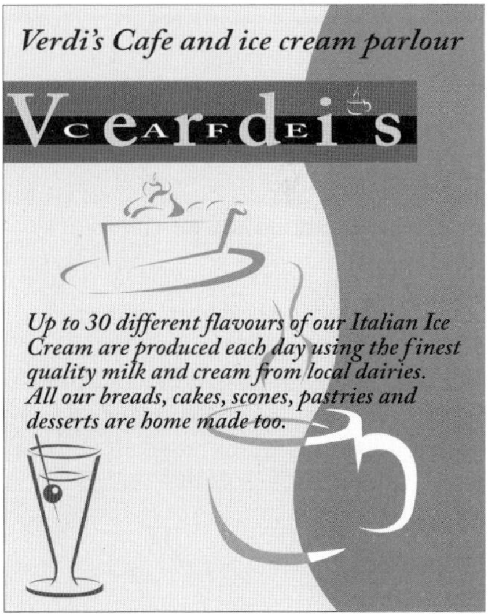
Verdi's Cafe and ice cream parlour
Verdi's
CAFE
Up to 30 different flavours of our Italian Ice Cream are produced each day using the finest quality milk and cream from local dairies. All our breads, cakes, scones, pastries and desserts are home made too.

PART 1: INTERVIEW

Good morning/afternoon. Welcome to your oral assessment. I hope you're fine. This is my colleague Mr Nguyen. He's just observing your performance. Please introduce yourselves.
My name's Chiara and I'm 16 years old. I'm from Gotha. I'm a pupil at Arnoldi Grammar School and I'm in Year 10.

Chiara, tell us a bit about your family.
Well, we are a family of five: my father and mother, my brother Marcus and my little sister Alexandra. My father works full-time and my mother part-time, my brother Marcus is a pupil at Arnoldi Grammar School, too. He's in Year 12. And my little sister still attends primary school.

[Vanessa, how do you share the housework?] And you, Chiara?
A lot of what Vanessa has said is true for our family, too. As both my parents go out to work, we all need to help at home. My mother does most of the work caring for us. She also does the cooking, the washing and the cleaning. But we all help in the kitchen. Alexandra usually lays the table and clears it. Marcus and I do the dishes and empty the dishwasher. My brother and I also have to clean our own rooms. My father usually does the work in the garden. To be honest, I think he should do more.

Chiara, how important is it for you and your parents to have meals together as a family?
Well, both my parents want us to have a meal in the evening together as a family. They are very strict about it because there's so little time when we are at home together as a family. At the weekend we also have lunch together. On Saturdays and Sundays my parents would like to have breakfast together with us, of course, but Marcus and I usually don't get up before 10 o'clock.

[Vanessa, how does your family celebrate festivities like Easter or Christmas?] And how does your family spend those times, Chiara?
We usually spend Easter and Christmas at home. We spend most of the time together as a family. My parents invite our grandparents and other relatives to our house or we go and see them. We sit together and eat and talk. On Easter Sunday and Boxing Day my grandparents traditionally invite their children and grandchildren out to dinner. That's good fun because we see all our aunts, uncles and cousins then.

Meals I usually have				
meal	**food I usually have**	**drinks**	**How healthy is what I …?**	
			eat	**drink**
breakfast	no food at all	milk, juice, tea	not good for my body	vitamins and minerals in milk and juice
snack at school	a sandwich, some fruit (apple, banana)	coke, lemonade	reasonably good	a lot of sugar – not good for my teeth or weight
lunch	hot meal with potatoes, meat, vegetables or soup dessert: yoghurt or fruit sometimes: lots of sweets instead	coke, lemonade	reasonably good unhealthy: a lot of sugar and fat, but no vitamins	see above
snack in the afternoon	piece of cake or sweets	coffee	see above	no vitamins
evening meal	bread, butter, sausage, cheese	tea	fatty, not enough vitamins	OK

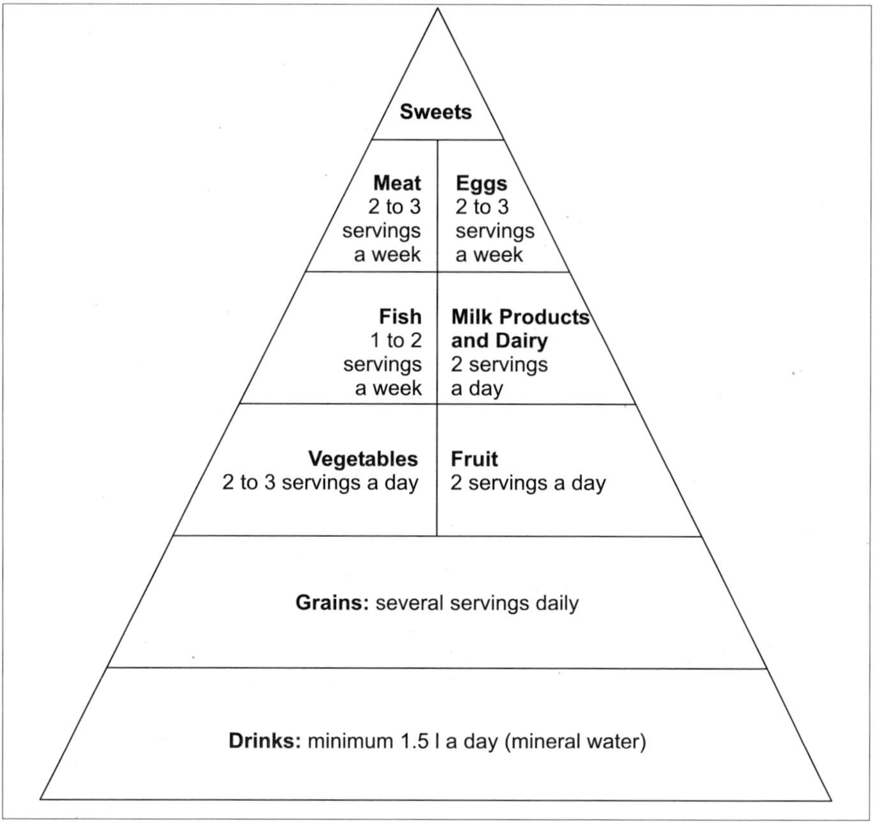

Example:

Hello everybody! I'd like to welcome you to my presentation. My task is to reflect on my eating habits and to explain what eating a healthy balanced diet actually means.

First let me tell you how I have structured my presentation. I will begin with my personal eating habits, talking about the meals I usually have. Second, I will discuss how healthy or unhealthy my eating habits are. I will find out if it is true for me that I eat too much fatty and sweet food, but not enough health food. Finally I will explain what eating a healthy balanced diet means.

Let me begin with the meals I usually have. I never have breakfast before I leave for school. I only have something to drink: a glass of milk or juice or a cup of tea. At school I usually have a sandwich and some fruit – mostly an apple or a banana. In the breaks I often buy some coke or lemonade. At about 12 o'clock I usually have lunch in the canteen: a hot meal with potatoes, some meat and vegetables, or soup. As dessert I often have a yoghurt or some fruit. But sometimes I don't like what's on offer and then I have a lot of sweets instead. At about 3 o'clock in the afternoon my mother comes home from work and we sometimes have some coffee and a piece of cake. For my evening meal I usually have some bread, sausage or cheese and a cup of tea.

Now I will discuss how healthy or unhealthy my eating habits are.

First, I suppose it is not very good for my body to leave for school on an empty stomach. On the other hand, I think the milk or juice I usually drink are a good start because of the vitamins and minerals. Second, in my opinion, the snack I have at school is reasonably good for me. But I'm afraid I consume too many sweet drinks at school. They contain a lot of sugar and therefore have a bad effect on my weight and teeth. I suppose I should try to drink mineral water or juice instead. Furthermore, the lunch I usually have at school is, again, reasonably good. But the problem is the sweets I sometimes have instead. Like sweet drinks, they are unhealthy because they do not have any vitamins, but instead contain a lot of sugar and often even a high amount of fat. I think I will definitely have to try to reduce the amount of sweets I eat to a minimum. Moreover, I am convinced I should be more careful about the sweet snack in the afternoon and I should have a healthier evening meal of fish, fruit or vegetables, and yoghurt and so on.

To sum up, I would say that it is probably true that I eat too much fatty and sweet food, but not enough health food.

I will now explain what eating a healthy balanced diet means.

Have a look at this picture. It shows some fruit and vegetables – a melon, pepper, lemon and an apple, a bottle labelled vitamins, a dumbbell and scales. The message of the picture is: if you want to stay fit and slim, you need to eat fruit and vegetables, take vitamins and exercise. What I do not like about the picture is the bottle labelled vitamins. Nowadays we know that vitamin pills do not always have a good effect on our bodies.

Anyway, let's have a look at the food pyramid. For a healthy balanced diet you should drink a lot every day – mainly mineral water. You should eat grains several times a day, like bread, cereals and pasta. Fruit, vegetables and milk and dairy products are also an important part of your diet and you should have them two or three times a day. You have to be a bit careful about the amount of meat and eggs you have and only eat them two to three times a week. But you can have fish instead once or twice. And last but not least, you must be very careful about the amount of sweets and sweet food you eat.

Finally, let's have a look at this cartoon. It shows the distances some foods travel before they end up on the table in an English Sunday lunch. Carrots, for example, are imported from South America and have travelled 9,620 kilometres before they get to the shops. Potatoes come from Italy and have travelled 2,447 kilometres before they are eaten. Beef is imported from Australia and the meat has travelled 21,462 kilometres before it is finally cooked. The cartoon shows very clearly the drawbacks that are connected with a healthy balanced diet. Food needs to be transported over long distances so that people can buy it in their local supermarkets whenever they like. The pollution of the environment is the price we pay for having fresh food, fruit and vegetables even in the winter. Is it worth it? Perhaps we should care more about where the food we eat comes from.

Let me close by saying that a healthy balanced diet is important for everyone. But it is equally important to start to think about whether we want to have fresh food, fruit and vegetables at any cost.

That was my presentation on my eating habits and on what eating a healthy balanced diet means. Thank you for your attention.

PART 3: TALK

Things you could talk about

Describe the menus:

- **Picture 1:** Italian restaurant; name: Olive Garden; Italian specialities (appetizers, soups and salads, pizzas, classic recipes, beef and pork, filled pastas, chicken, fish and sea food); some of the food is rather expensive, but some of it is affordable (pizza and pasta, for example)
- **Picture 2:** fast food menu (similar to McDonalds and Burger King); Quarter Pounders, chicken nuggets etc.; rather unhealthy (lots of sugar, fat and salt); the food is cheap
- **Picture 3:** Ruth's Steak House; offer high-quality steaks, but also other food like appetizers and soups, salads and sides, wine and cocktails and dessert
- **Picture 4:** café; name: Verdi's Café and Ice Cream Parlour; serve ice cream and homemade breads, cakes, scones, pastries and desserts; 30 different flavours of ice cream; mostly snacks and cold food

Personal preferences, e. g.

- What food do you like?
- Would you prefer a warm meal or just a snack?
- Do you like fast food or pizza?
- Are you a vegetarian or vegan?

Other aspects:

- Compare prices
- Is the food healthy?

PART 1: INTERVIEW

Teacher:

Good morning. Today is our oral assessment and we hope you are fine. This is my colleague Mr Lewandowsky. He is just going to listen to us. First of all, we would like to know something about you. Please introduce yourselves.

Farid, tell us about the last holiday you spent with your family.

And where did you go, Emma?

Farid: ...

Emma: ...

Do you already have plans for next summer?

What about you, Farid?

Emma: ...

Farid: ...

What tourist attraction would you suggest to someone who is on holiday in your hometown, Emma?

What about tourist attractions in your city, Farid?

Emma: ...

Farid: ...

SYDNEY: PART 2: PRESENTATION

Imagine you are just back from a three-week summer holiday in Australia. Now that school has started again, your teacher gives you the opportunity to talk about everything you have seen and learned. Present Australia as a tourist destination to your classmates.

Include the material from the presentation on www.stark-verlag.de/mystark.

You can arrange the pictures as you like.

PART 3: TALK

Teacher:
Now Emma and Farid, I'd like you to talk about a topic for 6 minutes. You will get some material to help you.
Now listen to your task carefully.

In this collage you can see different household gadgets. Discuss the necessity and advantages of these gadgets and decide on the most and least useful ones.

HOME CONTROL

PART 1: INTERVIEW

Good morning. Today is our oral assessment and we hope you are fine. This is my colleague Mr Lewandowsky. He is just going to listen to us. First of all, we would like to know something about you. Please introduce yourselves.
My name is Farid. I am 16 years old and I am from a village near Erfurt. I currently attend Year 10 here at Friedrich-Schiller high school.

Farid, tell us about the last holiday you spent with your family.
Last summer, I went to Majorca with my parents and my little brother. We took a plane from Berlin and spent two weeks having a good time at the beach. Our hotel was excellent: it was huge, the food was nice and it was all inclusive, so we could eat and drink whenever we felt like it. But the best thing was probably the surfing course I did during the two weeks. I really enjoyed it!

[Do you already have plans for next summer?]
What about you, Farid?
Staying in a hotel with my family like I did this year is nice, but I don't want to go on holiday with my parents anymore. I hope they let me spend one or two weeks with my two best friends. We are not sure where we want to go yet, but we thought that a camping trip would be great.

What about tourist attractions in your city, Farid?
Oh, the village I live in is so small, there are no great tourist attractions. I would probably tell them to visit Erfurt, which is near our village and where you can see the Krämerbrücke or the cathedral, for example.

PART 2: PRESENTATION

Hi everyone. As you know, I have been to Australia this summer. Today I want to show you what a great tourist destination it is and why it is worth a trip there.

Let me just give you a short overview of what I am going to talk about:

1. General facts
2. Animals
3. Nature

Let's begin ...

1. General facts:
   - Name: from word *australis* = southern, southern land
   - Nicknames: Oz, Down Under
   - Sixth largest country and whole continent
   - 2,500 miles wide, 7.7 million km^2
   - 80 % of population (21 million of about 25 million) live on coast
   - British monarch still head of state (but independent since 1901)

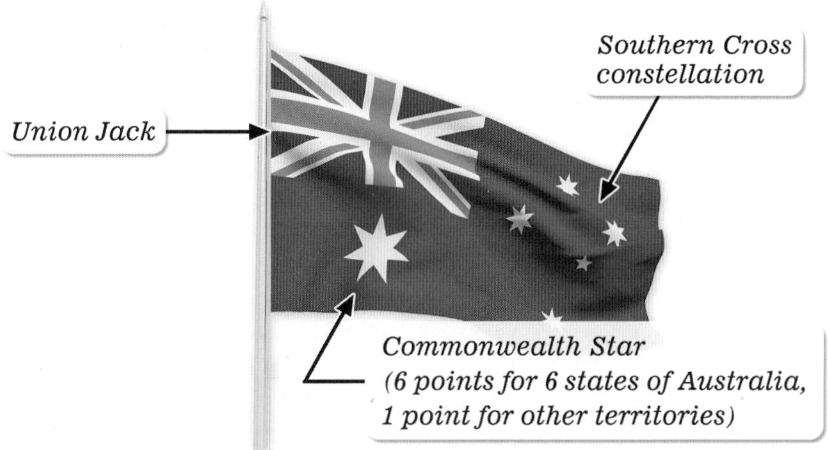

The Capital of Australia is Canberra. Other interesting cities are Melbourne, Brisbane, Perth and Adelaide. I only visited the city that seemed to be the most interesting to me: Sydney. In this picture you can see its skyline and its famous opera house.
If you don't like big cities so much but love animals or nature, Australia is the perfect holiday destination for you. I'll show you why.

2. Animals:
   - Three times as many sheep as people
   - Two times as many kangaroos as people
   - Termites, emus, platypus, koalas, camels ...
   - 21 of world's most poisonous snakes
   - Great Barrier Reef – go snorkelling, see thousands of colourful fish
     → Problem: global warming → water too warm → corals dying

3. Nature:
   - Surrounded by ocean → great variety of beaches → great for surfers
   - Pink lakes
   - Outback: deserts, rainforests → Aboriginals live there

One famous destination for visitors is Uluru or Ayers Rock. It is a sandstone rock formation that glows in the most wonderful colours, depending on the time of day. The area around it belongs to the Aboriginal people. We didn't climb the rock, because it is a sacred place for the Aboriginals and you're not allowed to go up it anymore. However, Uluru and all the other things I have shown you were wonderful, and I hope my presentation gave you an insight into this really exciting country.

Thank you for your attention.

PART 3: TALK

Things you could talk about

Gadgets in the kitchen:

- **Dishwasher:** not necessary because everyone has a sink to wash the dishes, but very good for saving time and water
- **Microwave:** not necessary – use stove to cook or warm up meals, advantage: warms up food very fast
- **Fridge:** necessary to keep food cold (especially meat, sausages)
- **Oven:** handy for baking and preparing a variety of meals, advantage: in contrast to using a stove, the oven does most of the work alone → time for other things

Other household gadgets:

- **Toothbrush:** don't necessarily need an electric one, but some claim that it cleans your teeth better
- **Iron:** useful for some kinds of clothes
- **Washing machine:** handy to wash lots of clothes in a short time, especially useful if a lot of people live in one household; washing by hand possible but nowadays no one would really do that anymore
- **Espresso machine:** not necessary – luxury item; lots of other drinks that can be drunk
- **Robot vacuum cleaner**: not necessary – normal vacuum cleaner sufficient too; not useful if there are stairs in your flat or house
- **Apps to control your household gadgets**: can be useful if you are on holiday and want to save energy, for example – turn gadgets (e. g. radiators) off when you leave and on shortly before you come back; **but:** potentially dangerous (e. g. broken oven, leaking washing machine)

In the end, don't forget to agree on the most and least useful gadget!

Aufgaben im Stil der BLF

Übungsaufgabe 4

PART 1: INTERVIEW

Teacher:

Good morning. Today is our oral assessment and we hope you are fine. This is my colleague Mr Gruber. He is just going to listen to us. First of all, we would like to know something about you. Please introduce yourselves.

Thank you. Now I'm going to ask you some more questions about yourselves.

Maja, please tell us about what an ordinary weekday is like for you.
What about you, Lucas?

Maja: ...
Lucas: ...

Do you sometimes have to help with the housework during the week?
And you, Maja?

Lucas: ...
Maja: ...

What gadgets do you usually use when you do housework?
Are there any other useful gadgets you use in your daily life, Lucas?

Maja: ...
Lucas: ...

PART 2: PRESENTATION

Technology can make everyday life easier and more comfortable. But it also has negative effects considering its influence on our environment and on people themselves. Discuss the pros and cons of modern technology.

Include the material from the presentation on www.stark-verlag.de/mystark.

You can arrange the pictures as you like.

PART 3: TALK

Teacher:
Now, Maja and Lucas, I'd like you to talk about a topic for 6 minutes. You will get some material to help you.
Now listen to your task carefully.

Your parents have allowed you to spend your next holidays with your best friend. Discuss the pros and cons of different kinds of holidays and agree on what you want to do together.

PART 1: INTERVIEW

Good morning. Today is our oral assessment and we hope you are fine. This is my colleague Mr Gruber. He is just going to listen to us. First of all, we would like to know something about you. Please introduce yourselves.
My name is Maja. I am 16 years old and I am a student in class 10b here at our school.

Thank you. Now I'm going to ask you some more questions about yourselves.
Maja, please tell us about what an ordinary weekday is like for you.
I usually get up at 6.30 in the morning. Then I get dressed, have breakfast and take the bus to school, where I stay until 2 pm. After school, I normally do my homework. If there is time afterwards, I meet my friends in the afternoon. My parents want me to be at home by 7.30 pm. That's when we usually have dinner. Most days I go to bed at 10 o'clock in the evening.

[Do you sometimes have to help with the housework during the week?]
And you, Maja?
Yes, I do. It is my job to take out the rubbish and vacuum every room in our house once a week. Those jobs are a bit annoying, but as everyone in our family has to do something in the household, I'm okay with it.

What gadgets do you usually use when you do housework?
I usually use the vacuum cleaner, because I have to vacuum the house. I am also glad that we have a dishwasher – I only have to empty it every other day instead of washing the dishes after every meal. And if it is my turn to cook at the weekend, I need the stove or the oven.

PART 2: PRESENTATION

Everyone has it, everyone needs it and everyone is dependent on it: technology. In this presentation I will talk about technology in different areas of life and discuss its pros and cons. Before I begin, let me tell you what structure I am going to use.

1. Technology in the household
2. Means of transport
3. Modern gadgets
4. Technology at the workplace and in science

Let's begin …

1. Technology in the household:
   (fridge, dishwasher, microwave, washing machine, vacuum cleaner)
   - Not possible to imagine living without them
   - Save time and money
   - Make life more comfortable

   but:
   - People get lazy (e. g. microwave instead of cooking → unhealthy)
   - Old gadgets use lots of energy
   - Huge problem if there is a power failure
2. Means of transport:
   (train, plane, electric car)
   - Travel around the world very fast
   - Makes people mobile
   - Transport goods (car: weekly shopping, plane: mail)

   but:
   - Not good for environment → air pollution
   - Planes especially need lots of fuel
   - E-mobility = step in right direction (but not enough people use it yet, not enough charging stations, high costs)
   - People get lazy (e. g. go by car instead of walking or riding a bike)
3. Modern gadgets:
   (laptop, smartphone, security camera, virtual reality glasses)
   - Laptop and smartphone: for work/homework, getting information quickly, staying in contact with friends from all over the world, finding one's route (GPS)
   - Security camera: people feel safer
   - Virtual reality glasses: explore and see things that usually wouldn't be accessible

   but:
   - Negative influence on social life (social media instead of meeting people in person, cyberbullying)
   - If smartphone gets lost/stolen or battery is low: people feel lost, some even panic → danger of addiction
   - Security cameras: people don't trust each other anymore, feel constantly controlled, privacy at risk
4. Workplace and science:
   - Machines are more precise, can carry heavier loads, don't need breaks

- Technology to discover more about the world, to send information around the world and make it accessible to everyone

but:

- People lose jobs in some fields of work if technology takes over

This is the end of my presentation. I hope I was able to show you in how many areas of life technology can be found and how dependent we are on it. Every kind of technology has its advantages but it is important not to forget what the negative side effects are. Despite the cons I talked about, I think that all in all the advantages of modern technology outweigh the disadvantages, and it is good that we have it.

PART 3: TALK

Things you could talk about

Holidays at the beach:

- **Pros:** relaxing, go swimming, enjoy beach parties, warm and sunny weather
- **Cons:** just lying around might get boring, sunburn, not enough action

Hiking and camping holidays

- **Pros:** lots of wonderful nature, active holidays, see many different places, spontaneous changes of plan possible, great atmosphere (sleep under the stars, have a campfire)
- **Cons:** not very relaxing, aching muscles, cold at night, weather might not be good, wild animals

Cruise:

- **Pros:** restaurants, bars, swimming pool, theatres on deck; visit many different places in short time, many different routes to choose from
- **Cons:** seasickness, small cabins, days at sea might be boring, bad for the environment, expensive

Sightseeing in a city:

- **Pros:** lots of sights, doesn't matter if weather is bad, many different activities possible
- **Cons:** too much hustle and bustle, no beach or place to relax if it's really warm

Skiing:

- **Pros:** combination of being in nature and having action, après-ski parties, many different trails
- **Cons:** many areas can't guarantee snow anymore, expensive, bad for the environment

Don't forget to agree on one kind of holiday that you want to do together!

Aufgaben im Stil der BLF
Übungsaufgabe 5

PART 1: INTERVIEW

Teacher:
Good morning. Today is our oral assessment and we hope you are fine. This is my colleague Ms Baumann. She is just going to listen to us. First of all, we would like to know something about you. Please introduce yourselves.

Thank you. Now I'm going to ask you some more questions about yourselves.

Anna, what are your favorite subjects and why?
How do you like English and Physics, Malek?

Anna: ...
Malek: ...

What things would you like to change at your school?
Do you agree with Malek, Anna?

Malek: ...
Anna: ...

Please tell me about your plans for when you leave school.
What do you want to do after you leave school, Malek?

Anna: ...
Malek: ...

PART 2: PRESENTATION

You are spending one year at an English boarding school. Your new classmates are interested in the differences between school in England and school in Germany. Present the most important differences to them and point out which advantages and disadvantages you see in the two school systems.

Include the given material.

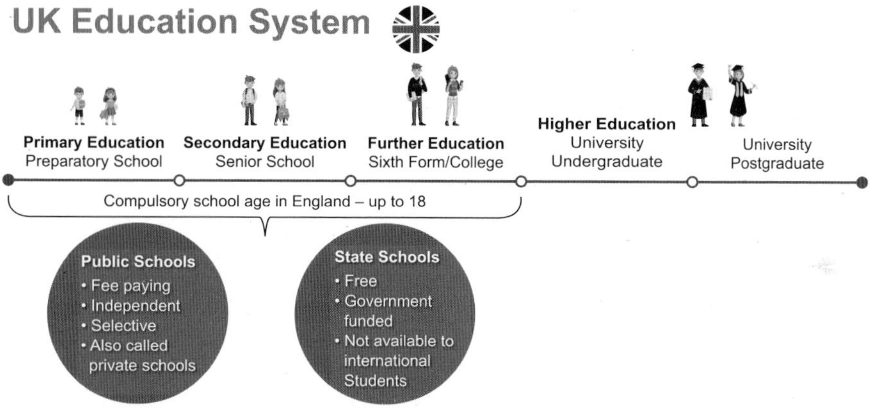

https://ukguardianship.com/uk-education-system-state-public-schools/

PART 3: TALK

Teacher:
It is never too late to think about the future. In these pictures you can see different jobs you could do after school. Discuss the qualities one must have for each job and then talk about your favourites.

PART 1: INTERVIEW

Good morning. Today is our oral assessment and we hope you are fine. This is my colleague Ms Baumann. She is just going to listen to us. First of all, we would like to know something about you. Please introduce yourselves.
My name is Anna. I am 16 years old and I live in Erfurt with my older sister and my mum.

Thank you. Now I'm going to ask you some more questions about yourselves.
Anna, what are your favourite subjects and why?
My favourite subjects are Physics and English. I love Physics because I always want to understand how things in our world work. We are discussing nuclear energy at the moment, for example. And since our last family holiday, I also appreciate English, because I've realised how cool it is to be able to talk to all kinds of people from different countries.

[What things would you like to change at your school?] Do you agree with Malek, Anna?
I wish we had more subjects or extracurricular activities to do with the arts. I like our music and art lessons, but I would like to sing in a choir or take part in a play or school musical.
And maybe we could do something about our school yard. I think it looks a bit grey and there isn't much to do in the breaks.

Please tell me about your plans for when you leave school.
I'm not sure yet what I want to study. At the moment, my plan is to go abroad for a year to do "work and travel". When we talked about Australia at school last year, I found the country very interesting and fascinating, so maybe I will go there.

PART 2: PRESENTATION

TIPP

Neben vorgegebenen Materialien, die du von deiner Lehrkraft bekommst und für eine Präsentation an der Tafel befestigst, kannst du eigene Dinge hinzufügen. Du könntest zum Beispiel deine Gliederung auf ein großes Blatt schreiben (Stifte und Blätter sollten im Vorbereitungsraum für dich bereit liegen). Das macht deine Präsentation für die Zuhörer*innen übersichtlicher und du hast eine Sache mehr, auf die du beim Sprechen verweisen kannst. **Zum Schluss musst du dir selbst eine Meinung bilden und diese in wenigen Sätzen zusammenfassen.**

My presentation is structured into the following parts:

1. kinds of schools and exams
2. public and state schools
3. other differences
4. positive and negative aspects of the two school systems

For my first point, let's have a look at this illustration.

1. kinds of schools and exams

Great Britain	Germany
primary education	**primary education**
• start school at age 5 • Years 1–6 • exams: SATs	• start school at age 6 or 7 • Years 1–4 (few exceptions) • no exams
secondary education	**secondary education**
• Years 7–11 (lower secondary) – Year 9: choose subjects for years 10 and 11 – exams: GCSEs • Years 12/13 (upper secondary) – Sixth Form/College (A-Levels) *or* • vocational training (preparation for full-time employment)	• Years 5–10 • split into *Gymnasium, Realschule* and *Hauptschule* (or *Gesamtschule*) • exams: *Hauptschulabschluss* (usually after year 9) or *Realschulabschluss* (after Year 10) • years 11/12 or 12/13 • exams: Abitur
higher education	**higher education**
• university	• university

2. public and state schools

in Great Britain:	
state schools	**public schools (= private schools)**
• free • government founded • not for international students	• parents must pay fees • open to international students • don't have to follow the national curriculum
in Germany:	
→both forms can be found in Germany →privately owned schools of lesser importance than in other countries →all schools overseen by state	

3. other differences

in Great Britain:	in Germany
• school uniforms • 3 terms • longer school holidays between each term • school = compulsory until 16; education until 18 • students cannot/don't have to repeat a year	• no school uniforms • 2 terms • more but shorter school holidays • school = compulsory until Year 9, education until 18/19 • sometimes pupils have to repeat a year

4. positive and negative aspects of the two school systems

   Before I come to the end of my short presentation, let me tell you what I like about the school systems and where I think there are disadvantages.

   Things you could talk about:

   - Is it an advantage or disadvantage that children start school at an earlier age in Great Britain?
   - In Germany, children are split into different groups (Gymnasium, Realschule and Hauptschule) at an early age. Do you think this is a good idea?
   - What about the role of private schools?
   - Is it an advantage or disadvantage that you have to wear school uniform in GB?
   - …

All in all, I can say that I really like it here and it makes me a bit sad that my exchange in England is almost over. Thank you for listening.

PART 3: TALK

> **TIPP**
>
> Ihr solltet unbedingt auf die vorgegebenen Bilder eingehen. Es ist darüber hinaus aber auch erlaubt, noch eigene Ideen einzubringen. Gefällt euch also keiner der abgebildeten Berufe, sagt das im Gespräch und bringt weitere Möglichkeiten für eure Zukunftsgestaltung ins Spiel.

Things you could talk about

As a **police officer** you need to be…
- self-confident
- responsible
- athletic
- able to deal with conflict
- a team player
- …

As a **secretary/accountant** you need to be…
- communicative
- autonomous
- accurate
- reliable
- able to cope with stress
- …

As a **lab technician** you need to be…
- precise
- neat
- patient
- good at abstract reasoning
- …

As a **kindergarten/nursery school teacher** you need to be…
- fond of children
- patient
- caring
- creative

…

Other things you can discuss:
- What are your personal strengths?
- Can you imagine doing one of the four jobs? Why/Why not?
- Is there another job you would like to do later?
- Have a guess: what do you think your partner would be good at?

Aufgaben im Stil der BLF
Übungsaufgabe 6

PART 1: INTERVIEW

Teacher:
Good morning. Today is our oral assessment and we hope you are fine. This is my colleague Ms Steube. She is just going to listen to us. First of all, we would like to know something about you. Please introduce yourselves.

Thank you. Now I'm going to ask you some more questions about yourselves.

Erik, tell me about your family's TV viewing habits.
Is that similar in your family, Ida?

Erik: ...
Ida: ...

Apart from the TV, what other media do you use?
What about you, Ida?

Erik: ...
Ida: ...

How often do you read and what kind of things do you read?
And you, Erik?

Ida: ...
Erik: ...

PART 2: PRESENTATION

Modern media are becoming part of people's lives more and more. Talk about the influence the media have on young people especially.

Include the given material.

"I thought I'd be a successful blogger by now."

PART 3: TALK

Here are some pictures about social media platforms. Speculate which platform they refer to and discuss positive and negative aspects of using social media.

Lösungsvorschläge

PART 1: INTERVIEW

Good morning. Today is our oral assessment and we hope you are fine. This is my colleague Ms Steube. She is just going to listen to us. First of all, we would like to know something about you. Please introduce yourselves.
My name is Erik. I'm going to be 16 years old in two weeks. I have an older brother and two younger sisters. We live with our parents in a village near Eisenach.

Thank you. Now I'm going to ask you some more questions about yourselves.
Erik, tell me about your family's TV viewing habits.
We usually watch the news together at 8 o'clock in the evening. Afterwards, my parents choose a programme – most days it's some kind of music programme. At the weekends, my sisters are allowed to stay up and watch with them, but during the week they have to go to bed. My brother and I usually watch something else on Netflix.

Apart from the TV, what other media do you use?
Well, I think what I use most is my smartphone. I have all my social media apps on it, I can watch videos on YouTube or google information for my homework. The other media I use are my laptop, my tablet and, of course, my PlayStation.

[How often do you read and what kind of things do you read?]
And you, Erik?
I like reading novels. It doesn't matter to me whether it's a love story or detective novel, as long as the plot is exciting. I usually start a new book when the school holidays are longer. During the school year I don't have so much time to read anything apart from books for German.

PART 2: PRESENTATION

TIPP

Je nachdem wie dein Fazit am Ende ausfällt, kannst du die Punkte 1 und 2 tauschen. Alternativ ist es auch möglich, immer ein positives und ein negatives Argument im Wechsel zu nennen.

These days, young people get in contact with social media and dream of becoming influencers at a very early age. The cartoon makes fun of this by showing two children on the playground. The little girl is rather disappointed that she has not managed to become a successful fashion blogger yet, which seems ridiculous as she is still a small child. On the other hand, many famous influencers on Instagram or TikTok are still teenagers or even children. Does this mean that early contact with social media is an advantage for children's future careers? And what are the downsides to excessive use of social media? It is these influences that I want to talk about in the next five minutes.

structure:

1. Positive influences of modern media
2. Negative influences of modern media
3. Summary – are modern media good or bad?

1. Positive influences of modern media
   - learning (with YouTube, Google, school apps, news media …)
   - exchanging information (class-chat, learning platforms …)
   - staying in a good mood (listening to music, funny clips on YouTube, games, social media apps …)
   - finding routes (GPS, Google Maps …)
   - developing and keeping up friendships (Facebook, WhatsApp, Instagram, Snapchat …)
   - improving skills (e. g. writing skills by starting your own blog)
   - …
2. Negative influence if people …
   - don't have any real-life contacts anymore
   - waste their time on apps and games (bad marks at school)
   - are not aware of media influence (advertising; violent behaviour, language or specific body images depicted as "normal")
   - don't think about what they read or see → believe fake news
   - use it to bully people (cyberbullying)
   - are victims of cyberbullying
   - get addicted
   - …
3. All in all, I think that …

   Things you could talk about:
   - Do the advantages of modern media outweigh the disadvantages?
   - What could/should be done to minimise the negative effects?

PART 3: TALK

Things you could talk about

The pictures refer to Instagram, TikTok, Facebook and Snapchat.

Positive aspects of social media:

- keep in contact with people from all over the world
- share important moments in your life with others
- fun and entertainment
- spread information very quickly to a wide audience
- …

Negative aspects of social media:

- cyberbullying, unwanted sexting
- private information can get into wrong hands
- spreading of fake news
- addiction
- people spend less time face to face
- …

Other things you might talk about:

- Which of these social media do you use? When? How often?
- Are there any platforms missing from the collage?
- All in all, would you say the advantages outweigh the disadvantages?
- Do you often think about negative aspects?

Aufgaben im Stil der BLF
Übungsaufgabe 7

PART 1: INTERVIEW

Teacher:
Good morning. Today is our oral assessment and we hope you are fine. This is my colleague Ms Weber. She is just going to listen to us. First of all, we would like to know something about you. Please introduce yourselves.

Thank you. Now I'm going to ask you some more questions about yourselves.

What kind of sports are you interested in and why?
Do sports play a role in your free time, Samira?

Theo: …
Samira: …

What role do your friends play in your free time?
What free time activities do you usually do with your friends, Samira?

Theo: …
Samira: …

Speaking of going out, Theo, please tell me about your plans for next weekend.
Do you have similar plans, Samira?

Theo: …
Samira: …

PART 2: PRESENTATION

The amount of free time young people have and the kind of activities they do change with every generation. Reflect on the changes that have taken place over the last few years. Then talk about popular activities of your age group and your own hobbies.

Include the given material.

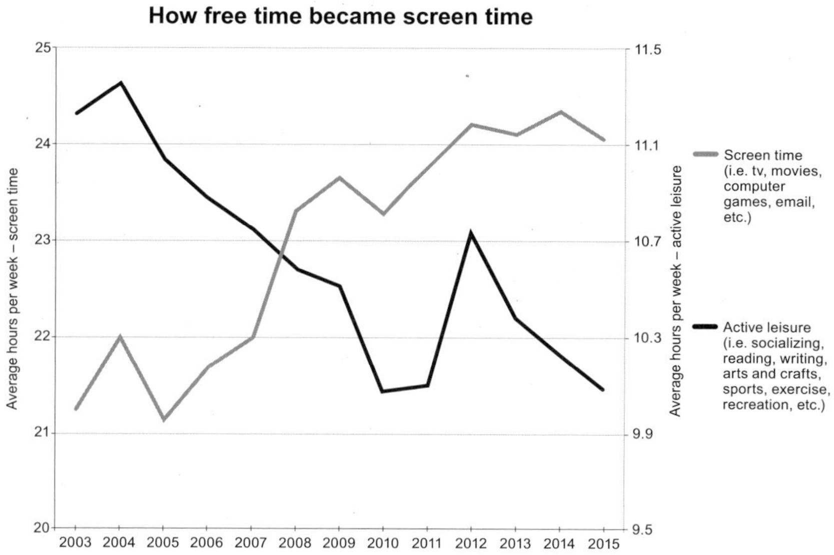

Source: Bureau of Labor Statistics 2013–2015 ATUS-CPS

PART 3: TALK

Caring for your own pet can be a wonderful leisure activity. Have a look at these pictures. First, discuss the pros and cons of keeping these animals and then decide on the one you would like to have.

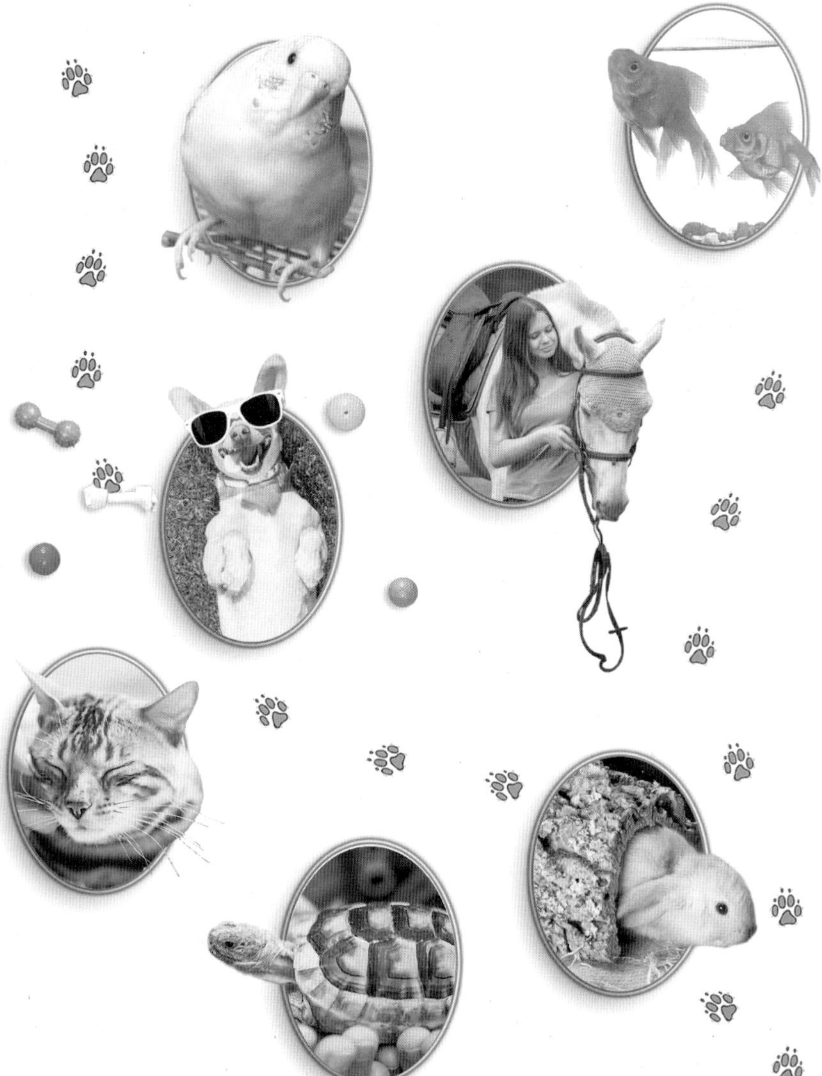

PART 1: INTERVIEW

Good morning. Today is our oral assessment and we hope you are fine. This is my colleague Ms Weber. She is just going to listen to us. First of all, we would like to know something about you. Please introduce yourselves.
My name is Theo. I am 16 years old and I live in Weimar. I am currently in Year 10 and my favourite subjects are PE and Geography.

Thank you. Now I'm going to ask you some more questions about yourselves.
What kind of sports are you interested in and why?
I am interested in football. I play for our local team and I think it's a great way to keep fit. Apart from that I like watching Champions League on TV and playing "FIFA" on my PlayStation. I like the fact that it's a team sport and that as a football fan you are never alone.

What role do your friends play in your free time?
Friends are extremely important to me. Without my football mates it wouldn't be possible to do the sport I love and without my other friends from school, going out would be boring.

Speaking of going out, Theo, please tell me about your plans for next weekend.
As our exams are over at the end of this week, I'm going to have a party with my friends. We are planning to meet in our garden because there are no parents to keep an eye on us all the time. We want to have a barbecue, listen to music and stay up late.

PART 2: PRESENTATION

It's the best time of the day, no matter whether you are 16, like me, or an adult: free time. In this presentation I want to talk about how leisure activities have changed over the last few years and then put the focus on activities of my own age group.

Before I start, I will give you an overview of the structure of my presentation.

1. Changes since 2003
2. Popular leisure activities of my generation
3. My own hobbies

1. Changes since 2003

   Let's start with my first point with the help of this diagram.

active leisure time:

- socialising, reading, writing, arts, crafts, recreation …
- dramatic decline between 2003 and 2011
- increase in 2012, then decline again

screen time:

- TV, movies, computer games, emails …
- huge increase between 2003 and 2015

possible reasons:

- rapid development of modern media
- better technical conditions (faster internet, not only computers but smartphones, tablets, etc.)
- flat rates and WiFi
- …

2. Popular leisure activities of my generation

   Modern media devices are also available in all price categories, which is the reason why from a young age, almost everyone has got at least a smartphone. Those devices are used all the time and therefore influence people's free time, too – especially people in my generation. This brings me to my second point.

   - Which media do your generation use?
   - Which apps/games … are popular?
   - How much free time is actually screen time in your generation?
   - How do you think the diagram has changed between 2015 and now?
   - Are there other popular activities that come under the category of active leisure?
   - …

3. My own hobbies

   I (don't) spend my free time like a typical teenager.

   - What are your hobbies?
   - How much screen time do you have per day?
   - What role do your friends play in your free time?
   - …

   As a conclusion, I want to say that …

   - What do you think about the development of active leisure time and screen time?
   - (positive, negative, surprising, …)
   - Should people change the way they spend their free time?
   - Will you rethink how you use your time?

PART 3: TALK

Things you could talk about

	pros	cons
dog	like a "best friend", helps you to get a lot of fresh air and to keep fit because of regular walks	has to be trained, barking may annoy neighbours, expensive (food, veterinary care)
horse	helps you to be active, riding improves balance and coordination, can help to reduce stress	expensive (food, vet exams, vaccinations), you need lots of space
cat	very clean, keep house and garden free of mice, can be left alone for a few days, can be kept inside an apartment but also left outside	dead mice on your doorstep, damage furniture, strong will (don't listen to commands like dogs)
budgie	can be taught to mimic speech, can be kept in small flats, not as expensive as other pets	can be very noisy, you usually have to buy at least two to keep them happy, you need a big cage or have to let them fly around at home (bird droppings, feathers)
rabbit	cuddly, quiet, don't need much space	like to bite and chew on everything, cage needs cleaning
fish	inexpensive, fish tank looks decorative, available in all sizes, relaxing to watch	cleaning the tank is a lot of work, can die easily (wrong water temperature, eat each other …)
turtle	independent – you don't need to go on walks with them, quiet, not picky concerning food, long lifespan	can't cuddle or play with them, all turtles carry salmonella, which they could pass on to you, need land and water
	→ you are never alone → you learn to take responsibility	→ you need money to buy your pet/food/other equipment → caring for a pet is time-consuming → you need so. to look after pets if you want to go on holiday

Which of these animals would you like to have? Why?
(And if you already have a pet: is there any other animal you could imagine keeping?)

Bildnachweis

S. 2 Schüler: Dean Drobot. Shutterstock, Fahrradunfall: Dmitrii Shironosov. 123rf.com; S. 6 Katarzyna Białasiewicz. 123rf.com; S. 8 Paul Jenkinson; S. 10 essende Frau: Matthew Ennis. Shutterstock, Sportlerin: sirtravelalot. Shutterstock, Frau mit Smartphone: Rawpixel.com. Shutterstock; S. 11 Flugzeug: ssuaphotos. Shutterstock, Hacker: subbotina. 123rf.com; S. 12 Wavebreak Media Ltd . 123rf.com; S. 17 Paul Jenkinson; S. 19 BlueSky-Image. Shutterstock; S. 20 agencyby. 123rf.com; S. 25 Schild „No“: Eric Crama. Shutterstock, Frau auf Demonstration: Jacob Lund. Shutterstock; S. 31 Kletterer: Leremy. Shutterstock, Schild: okeen. 123rf.com, Skateboarder: huhulin. 123rf.com; S. 34 Angonoa/Cartoonstock.com; S. 35 Rafting: Ammit Jack. Shutterstock, Skateboarderin: lzf. Shutterstock, Mädchen beim Klettern: Sergey Novikov. Shutterstock, Mountainbike: Warren Goldswain. Shutterstock, Taucherin: Dudarev Mikhail. Shutterstock; S. 37 Randy Glasbergen, www.glasbergen.com; S. 54 © Piotr Paczynski/Dreamstime.com; S. 60 New York: Andrey_Popov. Shutterstock, Fahrzeuge: MAKSIM ANKUDA. Shutterstock, Rakete: kornn. Shutterstock, Kopfhörer: Jane Kelly. Shutterstock, Rasenmäher: Mr_Vector. 123rf.com; S. 61 links oben: © Helen Filatova/Dreamstime.com, rechts oben: © Joegough/Dreamstime.com, links unten: © Juri Bizgajmer/Dreamstime.com, rechts unten: © Thierry Maffeis/Dreamstime.com; S. 76 Sydney: Hannah Jessup. 123rf.com, Surfer: EpicStockMedia. Shutterstock, Fische: Brian Kinney. Shutterstock, Yugambeh Aboriginal Man Boomerang: rafaelbenari. 123rf.com; S. 77 Spülmaschine: dibrova. Shutterstock, Microwelle: Africa Studio. Shutterstock, Zahnbürste: Alliance. Shutterstock, Toaster: SeDmi. Shutterstock, Espressomaschine: bartkowski. 123rf.com, Bügeleisen: Phasin Sudjai. 123rf.com, Staubsaugerroboter: Andrey Bryzgalov. Shutterstock, Waschmaschine: Sashkin. Shutterstock, Kühlschrank: ppart. Shutterstock, App: Kittaya Mangruan. 123rf.com; S. 79 Gil C. Shutterstock; S. 82 Spülmaschine: dibrova. Shutterstock, Autos: sungsu han. Shutterstock, Laptop: Valeria Aksakova. Shutterstock, Satellit: fstockfoto. Shutterstock; S. 83 Strand: Syda Productions. Shutterstock, Wandern: My Good Images. Shutterstock, Urlaubsplanung: Sebnem Ragiboglu. 123rf.com, Skifahren: Jan Novak. 123rf.com, Zelt: Studio 1One. Shutterstock, Kreuzfahrt: rawpixel. 123rf.com; S. 88 Zeichnungen in Grafik: Tartila. Shutterstock, Schuluniform: Cathy Yeulet. 123rf.com, Gruppe auf Campus: Joana Lopes. Shutterstock; S. 89 Polizistin: John Roman Images. Shutterstock, Geschäftsmann: Elnur. Shutterstock, Wissenschaftlerin: PhotoSky. 123rf.com, Erzieher: oliveromg. Shutterstock, S. 95 Cartoon: Bruce Kaplan/Cartoonstock.com, Millennials: Cathy Yeulet. 123rf.com; S. 96 Smartphone: Various-Everythings. Shutterstock, Template (instant photo): estherpoon. 123rf.com, schwarze Frau: And-One. Shutterstock, Mädchen mit Sonnenbrillen: View Apart. Shutterstock, Hundegesichter: BlueRingMedia. Shutterstock, Mädchen mit Emojis: rawpixel. 123rf.com, Social Media: primagefactory. 123rf.com, Mädchen (Mobbing): oliveromg. Shutterstock, singende Mädchen (links): Shutterstock, singende Mädchen (rechts): silverkblackstock. Shutterstock; S. 102 Fußballspielerinnen: wavebreakmedia. Shutterstock, Freund*innen: fizkes. Shutterstock, Computerspiele: sezer66. Shutterstock, Bücherleser: Prudencio Alvarez. 123rf.com; S. 103 Wellensittich: VitCOM Photo. Shutterstock, Fische: LUIS PADILLA-Fotografia. Shutterstock, Pferd: sheiko. 123rf.com, Hund: damedeeso. 123rf.com, Katze: PHOTOCREO Michal Bednarek. Shutterstock, Kaninchen: Anna Schram. 123rf.com, Schildkröte: loocmill. Shutterstock